THE TRUTH
WILL SET YOU FREE

THE TRUTH
WILL SET YOU FREE

11 "Myths" Satan Uses to Deceive Man

Robert W. Sayre Sr.

PR**I**MIX
PUBLISHING
THE WRITE CHOICE

Primix Publishing
East Brunswick Office Evolution
1 Tower Center Boulevard, Ste 1510
East Brunswick, NJ 08816
www.primixpublishing.com
Phone: 1-800-538-5788

Published by Primix Publishing: 01/13/2025

ISBN: 979-8-89194-383-4(sc)
ISBN: 979-8-89194-384-1(e)

Library of Congress Control Number: 2024924978

CONTENTS

ACKNOWLEDGEMENT

This book would not be possible without the bible knowledge learned through BSF, Bible Study Fellowship. BSF is a free, non-domination, international bible study. They reinforces God's message in four ways:

1. A daily reading of a small section of the bible book you are studying and answering questions.

2. A 45 minute discussion with a small group of peers about the weeks questions you and you're your piers answered.

3. A 40 minute large group lecture on the material you read, answered questions on and discussed with your peers.

4. Upon leaving you receive 6 pages of inspired notes about the material you read and answered questions on, you discussed with your peers and listened to a great lecture. Your first day's assignment is to answer questions on the lecture and the notes.

There are separate BSF classes for adult men and women plus coed classes for young single men and women. All local BSF staff members are volunteers and lay people dedicated to spreading God's truth through His inspired Word, the bible. BSF avoids petty differences in dominations and focuses on Jesus Christ the "Savior of the World". None of this would be possible without dedicated God fearing volunteers who deserve my thanks and gratitude:

1. Mark Simpson, the men's teaching leader in St Louis, who dedicated much of his life for the past ten plus years organizing and teaching St Louis' men's BSF class. Mark also holds a separate leader's meeting each Saturday morning, and delivers a 40+ minute lecture every Tuesday evening for 30+ weeks each year to about 500 hundreds of men seeking a relationship with God/Jesus.

2. Jim Miller, the previous children programs administer for many years is now the BSF administrator. I worked under Jim's guidance for seven years as a children's leader. Jim is also a dedicated man of God whose time and organization makes BSF in St Louis run smoothly.

3. Teaching leaders are also an essential part of BSF and are responsible for keeping a personal relationship with their 10-15 men they mentor each week. They must attend a weekly leaders meeting, communicate with each member prior to class, pray for members concerns and keep the discussion group on track and on time.

4. BSF's headquarters staff in San Antonia, , writes and publishes the great notes and questions all members worldwide receive. Much of the everyday labor is also done through volunteers from all over the world. However, they have a permeate staff of well-educated Spirit led Christians involved in the production of all the BSF study material.

I thank God for Mark Simpson, Jim Miller and the numerous discussion leader for their time and dedication in promoting God's truth about Jesus who is "the way the <u>truth</u> and the life" BSF gave me a hunger to seek out God's truth and answered the most important questions about sin, mercy, grace, faith, eternal life and most of all, salvation!

ABOUT THE AUTHOR

The author has been in intense Bible studies for the past forty years including over twenty five tears in BSF, Bible Study Fellowship. He just published a book, "Mankind is Without Excuse." Faith is required to believe in Creation vs Evolution.

INTRODUCTION

What is truth? Webster's dictionary defines truth: *"1: TRUTHFULINESS, HONESTY 2: the real state of things: FACT 3: the body of real evidence or facts: ACTUALITY."*

My main intent in writing this book is to use God's Word, the Bible, to distinguish between God's truth and Satan's seductive deceptions. The Bible is God's "Use and Care Manual" for our abundant life here on earth and for eternity. Every person is either lost or saved and will live in either in Heaven or Hell for eternity, Therefor, it is essential that we know the truth in the Bible regarding the most important issues affecting our lives here on earth and more importantly for eternity. Matthew 16:26 *"What good will it be for someone to gain the whole world, yet forfeit their soul? Or what can anyone give in exchange for their soul?*

The Bible talks about a time on earth when men will abandon God's word and follow their own way; they will rationalize immorality and deviant behavior. 2 Timothy 4:3-4 *"For the time will come when people will not put up with sound doctrine. Instead, to suit their own desires, they will gather around them a great number of teachers to say what their itching ears want to hear.* ⁴ *They will turn their ears away from the truth and turn aside to myths."* I believe that time has finally come.

What you believe has eternal consequences. Satan does not want you to know God's truth and be set free from sin's bondage and death. John 3:36 *"Whoever believes in the Son has eternal life, but whoever* rejects the Son will not see life, for God's wrath remains on them." Belief in God is only the 1ˢᵗ step in having a relationship with God as even the demons believe in God. James 2:19 *"You believe that there is one God. Good! Even the demons believe that—and shudder."*

Satan uses logic, emotion, and opinions of others to lead us astray. We must trust only in God's inspired Word, the Bible, for real truth. When a passage in the Bible is not clear or seems to contradict God's Word, find other passages that are clearer on the subject. Proverbs 14:12 *"There is a way that appears to be right to a man, but in the end it leads to death."*

God's word is mocked, distorted and lied about continuously. Satan and his followers want to remove even the mention God/Jesus from everything everywhere. Their lies/distortions will cost them dearly in eternity but they also lead many others astray. Heaven has no place for liars as they are equated with murderers, the cowardly, the unbelieving and the vile. Revelations 21:8 *"But the cowardly, the unbelieving, the vile, the murderers, the sexually immoral, those who practice magic arts, the idolaters and all liars—they will be consigned to the fiery lake of burning sulfur. This is the second death."*

Today the secular world blurs the true meaning of truth. They believe that what is true for you may not be the same as what is true for me. Blurring truth is not new as Satan has been bending the truth ever since the fall of man in the Garden of Eden. Satan lied about what God actually said to Adam and Eve. Genesis 2:16-17 *"And the Lord God commanded the man, "You are free to eat from any tree in the garden; ¹⁷ but you must not eat from the tree of the knowledge of good and evil, for when you eat from it you will certainly die."* Satan's lie and Adan and Eve's disobedience has caused the death and decay of everything ever since. Genesis 3:4-5 *"You will not certainly die," the serpent said to the woman. ⁵ "For God knows that when you eat from it your eyes will be opened, and you will be like God, knowing good and evil."*

Man's eyes were opened to the" knowledge of good and evil". However, death to every living thing was an extremely high price to pay for that knowledge. The knowledge of evil has drawn man into continuous sin/disobedience ever since Adam and Eve's disobedience. Today, sin is beyond man's ability to resist by his own power!

Satan has been successful as secularism has taking over and promoted by the main stream media, our public schools, our universities, our state and local governments and even in many Christian Churches today. In regard to churches, there is an old saying: ***"Churches that stand for nothing will fall for anything"***!

Unfortunately many churches have compromised Gods truth in order to attract more members. They have sold out to the secular world by compromising the truth in scripture which clearly states sins damming effect on man. They ignored the" just wrath" of God which is also a part of His character. <u>Romans 2:5</u> ***"But because of your stubbornness and your unrepentant heart, you are storing up wrath against yourself for the day of God's wrath, when his righteous judgment will be revealed."*** <u>Hebrews 10:30-31</u> ***"For we know him who said, "It is mine to avenge; I will repay," and again, "The Lord will judge his people, It is a dreadful thing to fall into the hands of the living God."***

Sin is man's terminal illness, but faith/belief in Jesus the Christ is God's only antidote! All God's promises hinge on having faith/belief. However, the other ingredient to being a true Christin is obedience to His teaching. <u>John 8:31-32</u> ***"Jesus said, "If you hold to my teaching, you are really my disciples. ³² Then you will know the truth, and the truth will set you free."*** <u>John 14:21</u> ***"Whoever has my commands and keeps them is the one who loves me. The one who loves me will be loved by my Father, and I too will love them and show myself to them."***

Jesus is the absolute truth! <u>John 14:6</u> ***"I am the way, <u>the truth</u> and the life. No one comes to the father except me".*** Satan is at the opposite end of truth and deceives man by bending the truth just enough be believed by most people. Satan, on the other hand is the author of lies! <u>John 8:34</u> ***"You belong to your father, the devil, and you want to carry out your father's desires. He was a murderer from the beginning, not holding to the truth, for there is no truth*** *in him. When he lies, he speaks his native language, for he is a liar and the father of lies."*

Even many pastors/priests bend God's truth by stating that God loves everyone "unconditionally". Many church members after hearing this message will have one or two of the following responses:

1. If God loves me "unconditionally", then He doesn't care what sins I commit or how I live my life, therefore all people will go to heaven.

2. Logic and personal experience in day to day life, raises serious questions regarding God's "unconditional love" because of wars, natural disasters, sickness, death of a loved one etc.

The above responses will sow seeds of doubt in people's minds regarding the truth of scripture. Chapter #5 clearly illustrates that God loves His children unconditionally but certainly not everyone!

Another major myth believe by most Christians is that God gave us "freewill" to choose Jesus as God didn't want us to be robots. Yes, God did give man freewill to sin and do almost everything except make a decision for Him and Jesus Christ. This myth causes pride in many believers. They take self-credit for their faith and think they are smarter than their non-believing sinful friends. Chapter #4 quotes over 100 verses in both the Old and New Testaments refuting that myth. Other chapters in my book also prove that my myths are actually, *myths*!

Christianity is different from all other religions. All other religion requires man to earn their salvation or Heaven. Only Christianity has God doing all the work. Jesus's suffering; death on the cross and His resurrection from the dead did all the work required for man to enter Heaven. Jesus took our sinfulness and exchanged it with His righteousness. All we have to do is believe in Him and what He did for us. All that is required from us is faith or belief which comes by knowing God/Jesus personally.

Pleasing God begins with faith. Hebrews 11:6 *"And without faith it is impossible to please God, because anyone who comes to him must believe that he exists and that he rewards those who earnestly seek him."* How do we strengthen our faith? Romans 10:17 *"Consequently, faith comes from hearing the message, and the message is heard through the word about Christ".* God's use and care manual was given to man so we could know Him and have an intimate relationship with Him. If you don't know the rules of life, written by man but inspired by God, then how can you possibly please God, our creator?

The good news is that God promises wisdom to anyone who asks. James 1:5-8 *"If any of you lacks wisdom, you should ask God, who gives generously to all without finding fault, and it will be given to you. ⁶ But when you ask, you must believe and not doubt,*

because the one who doubts is like a wave of the sea, blown and tossed by the wind.

⁷ That person should not expect to receive anything from the Lord. ⁸ Such a person is double-minded and unstable in all they do. Doubt is the opposite of faith!

When seeking the truth about God, He promises if you seek him, He will be found! Matthew 7:7-8 *"Ask and it will be given to you; seek and you will find; knock and the door will be opened to you. ⁸ For everyone who asks receives; the one who seeks finds; and to the one who knocks, the door will be opened."* Chronicles 15:2 *"The LORD is with you when you are with him. If you seek him, he will be found by you, but if you forsake him, he will forsake you."*

God does not appreciate lukewarm Christians either. Revelations 3:15-16 *"I know your deeds, that you are neither cold nor hot. I wish you were either one or the other! ¹⁶ So, because you are lukewarm— neither hot nor cold—I am about to spit you out of my mouth."* Martin Luther King, Jr., once said: *"The hottest place in Hell is reserved for those who remain neutral in times of great moral conflict."* C.S. Lewis when talking about Christians who made their mark on this world by focusing on heaven: *"Aim at heaven and you will get earth thrown in. Aim at earth and you will get neither"*

Please, don't just accept my words, but check them out for yourself. The apostle Paul says that you should be like the "Bereans": Acts 17:11 *"Now the Berean Jews were of more noble character than those in*

Thessalonica, for they received the message with great eagerness and examined the Scriptures every day to see if what Paul said was true." A meaningful sign in front of a church read: "Dusty Bibles leads to dirty lives."

Seek God and He will be found! John 8:32 *"Then you will know the truth, and the truth will set you free."*

Cross references:

Revelation 21:8 : ver 27; Ps 5:6; 1Co 6:9; Heb 12:14; Rev 22:15

Revelation 21:8 : S Rev 9:17

Revelation 21:8 : S Rev 2:11

CHAPTER 1

THE TRUTH WILL SET YOU FREE

Don't Confuse me With Facts!

What is Truth?

Can something be true and false at the same time? Can something be true for you and false for someone else? If you believe there is a God and I deny that God exists, can we both be right? If you believe that The Bible "is" the Word of the "One and Only True God" and I believe in Evolution or the "God of Chance", can we both be right? The penalty for being wrong has eternal consequences!

Good lawyers always teach their clients to POP, "put on paper". Although verbal agreements are binding, they are harder to enforce because people may disagree on what was actually verbally agreed upon down the road. I believe God inspired men to put His instruction manual, the Bible, on paper so there would be no misunderstanding as to what God desires/demands of man. Even though man evolves and rationalizes his/her behavior over time, God/Jesus never changes His standards and is eternal.. Hebrews 13:8 *"Jesus Christ is the same yesterday and today and forever.*

Man gets into trouble when he changes or compromises God's law. The Roman Catholic Church did this when the Pope over ruled the Bible in order to sell "indulgences", a money raising scheme where the rich could buy their way into Heaven. This raised money to build the magnificent cathedrals during the middle ages. Today many churches ignore the Bible's teaching instead promote "name it and claim it" i.e., if you are a generous Christian and pray for your "greed's" not your "needs" you will lead a trouble free/abundant life. God's Word promises just the opposite. John 15:20 *"Remember what I told you: 'A servant is not greater than his master.' If they persecuted me, they will persecute you also."*

Two Classes of People on Earth

There are only two classes of people on earth, those who are saved and those who are lost. The saved are people who believe in God who created the Heaven and Earth and in Jesus His sinless Son. They believe that Jesus was crucified on a Roman cross, He died and rose from the dead in order to pay the price of our sinfulness. In God's eyes, Jesus exchanged His righteousness for our sinfulness. Because of Jesus death and resurrection, the saved will live forever in Heaven. John 5:24 *"Very truly I tell you, whoever hears my word and believes him who sent me has eternal life and will not be judged but has crossed over from death to life.*

The saved are God's children and are given His gift of His Holy Spirit. The Bible referees to them as "His chosen, His called, His appointed, His elect or those who were predestined" to spend eternity in Heaven with Him. Acts 13:48 *"and all who were appointed for eternal life believed."* Believing/faith are the essential ingredients to being one of God's children who are deemed righteous in God's eyes.

The lost are those who deny the existence of God and His Son are condemned and subject to God's wrath. John 3:18 *"Whoever believes in him is not condemned, but whoever does not believe stands condemned already because they have not believed in the name of God's one and only Son."* <u>2 Thessalonians 1:8-9</u> *"He will punish those who do not know God and do not obey the gospel of our Lord Jesus. ⁹ They will be punished with everlasting destruction and shut out from the presence of the Lord and from the glory of his might"*

Three Ways Man Decides What is True in Life

There are three basic influences that someone uses to makes a decision as to the truth about something.

1. A friend or someone in authority that they trust tells them what they believe as truth and they go along with his/her opinion. It might be a parent, a family member, a pastor, a radio or TV celebrity or someone that they believe is more knowledgeable than they are.

2. They have a "gut" feeling that a certain position is right. They trust their intuition as a   good way to decide right from wrong. Their decision is based on logic, reason, and what seems to be most loving or gracious.

3. They find their answers in the Bible. When one passage seems to be less clear or illogical, they look for other clearer passages to provide God's truth. If God's Word is at odds with their own intuition, or with those in authority, they trust God's Word as truth.

Most Christians want to know and do the right thing when it comes to their behavior. The only way to know what is actually true is to study God's word, the Bible! Do not put your faith in what other people claim to believe in or in what seems logical to you. <u>Proverbs 3:5</u> *"Trust in the Lord with all your heart and lean not on your own understanding;"* Trust only in God's word!

The early "Church" set out to reform the world and by following the example Jesus set before us in the New Testament. Unfortunately, the world has corrupted even the church and today, there is little difference between the actions of some so called saved vs. the lost.

Why Take a Chance? …. "Pascal's Wager"

Pascal's Wager is an argument in apologetic philosophy devised by the seventeenth-century French philosopher, mathematician and physicist Blaise Pascal (1623–62). It posits that humans all bet with their lives either that God exists or that he does not.

> *"God is, or He is not." But to which side shall we incline? Reason can decide nothing here. There is an infinite chaos which separated us. A game is being played at the extremity of this infinite distance where heads or tails will turn up… Which will you choose then? Let us see. Since you must choose, let us see which interests you least. You have two things to lose, the true and the good; and two things to stake, your reason and your will, your knowledge and your happiness; and your nature has two things to shun, error and misery. Your reason is no more shocked in choosing one rather than the other, since you must of necessity choose… But your happiness? Let us weigh the gain and the loss in wagering that God is… If you gain, you gain all; if you lose, you lose nothing. Wager, then, without hesitation that He is."*

In other words, if God exist and you believe in him you gain eternal life in heaven. If God doesn't exist and you believed in him you lose nothing. You may lose some short term pleasures/sin in this life, however, if God does exist and you reject Him you spend eternity in Hell.

Is the Bible Fact or Fiction?

Some believe that the Bible is just a bunch of stories handed down over 1000's of years which have been highly exaggerated over time. God inspired human writers through His Holy Spirit to give man a glimpse of His nature and offers a guide on how we are to live with Him eternally. Historically and archeologically, the Bible has been proven to be 100% accurate. No matter what you believe, you should have facts to support your beliefs. More importunately, our eternal life depends on being right about God as eternity is a long, long, long time!

The Holy Bible is a collection of 66 books written by man but was inspired by God. Unlike any other book, it was written by many different authors over 1,500 years in 3 languages, in numerous countries, on 3 continents and illustrates a consistent message of salvation as if it were written by one author.

God inspired the writers of the Bible in order to help man understand His character and how to live a righteous life:

1. 2 Peter 1:20-21 *"Above all, you must understand that no prophecy of Scripture came about by the prophet's own interpretation of things. [21] For prophecy never had its origin in the human will, but prophets, though human, spoke from God as they were carried along by the Holy Spirit."* God dictated the Bible through many different men over many years.

2. 2nd Timothy 3:16 *"All Scripture is God-breathed and is useful for teaching, rebuking, correcting and training in righteousness,"*

3. 1st Corinthians 2:13 *"This is what we speak, not in words taught us by human wisdom but in words taught by the Spirit, expressing spiritual truths in spiritual words."* We need God's Spirit in order to fully understand its meaning."

4. Proverbs 30-5-6 *"Every word of God is flawless; he is a*

shield to those who take refuge in him.[6] *Do not add to his words, or he will rebuke you and prove you a liar."*

God is omniscient and knows before you were born weather you are His child or a child of Satan. Psalm 139:16 *"all the days ordained for me were written in your book before one of them came to be."* Matthew 25:34 *"Then the King will say to those on his right, 'Come, you who are blessed by my Father; take your inheritance, the kingdom prepared for you since the creation of the world.*

God wants man to know Him as He is "truthfully" portrayed, not what sinful man rationalizes Him to be. Making God out to fit our idea of Him is "idol worship". Knowing God's truth is essential in order to understand God's sovereign nature. There are many myths that have grown up over time which must be exposed in order to truly know our Sovereign God. This book contains 11 myths about God's nature that I believe should be challenged.

Did man evolve over billions of years by chance? Does man have the ability to choose God on his own? Does God actually love "everyone unconditionally"? These are just a few of the key myths that this book attempts to expose. Please don't believe my words but seriously consider God's words in the greatest book ever written.

God Seeks Man Until Man Discovers God

God desires man to seek Him before considering anything else in regard to their life. Matthew 16:33 *"But seek first his kingdom and his righteousness, and all these things will be given to you as well."* Our desire to diligently seek God happens when we receives the Gift of His Holy Spirit or through the study of His Word. God created a natural void in everyone which must be filled with "faith or belief" in one of the following:

1. Belief in the "God of the Bible" and faith in what Jesus did for man on the cross is what Christianity is all about.

Belief in Jesus' suffering, death and resurrection for the forgiveness of our sins is what determines where man will spend eternity.

2. Belief in evolution or "false gods "which are the creation of man is "idol worship" and forbidden by God. Putting anything in front of God i.e. family, money, power etc. is "Idol Worship" may result in eternal death.

3. Our world is controlled by the" Satan, who is the "Prince of this World". John 12:31 *"Now is the time for judgment on this world; now the prince of this world will be driven out."* Satan and the world attempts to build up man and diminish God. Satan wants man to be self-centered rather God- centered, resulting in separation from God and eternal damnation

Throughout history man has taken God for granted. Faith grows more in difficult times rather than when everything is going smoothly. When things go well we tend to take credit for all of God's blessings. Unfortunately, God knows that we are more likely to come to Him when all else fails: Psalm 78:34 *"Whenever God slew them, they would seek him; they eagerly turned to him again."* Our prayer should be: Psalm 80:3 *"Restore us, O God; make your face shine upon us, that we may be saved"* Psalm 85:7 *"Show us your unfailing love, O LORD, and grant us your salvation."*

Satan is the Author of lies!

Satan, the accuser, has caused many people to question that God is the creator of the universe and is in complete control of everything. The truth is that God knows your every movement, your every thought before you speak them. God even knows the number of hairs on your head.

Satan has successfully infiltrated our universities, the main stream media, our government and even many of our churches. One of Satan greatest weapons is to convince people that God doesn't exist. Darwin's book on evolution created doubt about creation and the need for God. If man evolved by chance over billions of years then there is no God and therefore, no judgement for sinfulness so the person with the most toys wins. Unfortunately the belief that the earth and man was created by chance has been accepted as fact by many people today. **The only true fact regarding evolution is that it can not be proven scientifically!**

Satan and his followers also use intimidation as a weapon. Scientists who suggest that "intelligent design" may better explain creation than evolution are losing their jobs and being ridiculed by their peers. Ben Stein's movie *"EXPELLED"* goes into great detail in exposing what happens to scientists who even hint at the possibility of intelligent design. Believers who quote the Bible are accused of being religious zealots. Without knowing Gods Word, people tend to believe in evolution as fact, rather then what is at best only a scientific theory. Unless something can be duplicated or observed at best can be considered a theory!

Being chosen by God, called, His elect, or those predestined are referenced throughout the Bible. What do these words mean to you? Most believers have been taught that God gave us "free will" in order that we could choose him rather than being robots. Some denominations seem to reinforce this concept as it makes "The Church" essential in you make "a decision for Christ".

The church is an essential tool God uses to introduce His children to the Trinity, God the Father, God the Son and God the Holy Spirit. God desires them to grow closer to Him through sanctification. <u>Proverbs 27:17</u> *"As iron sharpens iron, so one person sharpens another."* We need the church and one another in order to resist the world's many temptations. Bible study is also very important in resisting Satan, and the world's temptations.

False Prophets

The most dangerous people on earth are the "false prophets", those who claim to know and believe in God but are wolves in sheep's clothing;

1. Matthew 7:15 *"Watch out for false prophets. They come to you in sheep's clothing, but inwardly they are ferocious wolves." They lie, intimidate and lead followers astray.*

2. Matthew 24:24 *"For false messiahs and false prophets will appear and perform great signs and wonders to deceive, if possible, even the elect."* False prophets may be your friends or possibility even religious leaders.

3. Acts 20:30 *"Even from your own number men will arise and distort the truth in order to draw away disciples after them."* If we lose our life defending Christianity, we will spend eternity in Heaven with Jesus, but if we deny Him we spend eternity in Hell.

4. Matthew 10:28 *"Do not be afraid of those who kill the body but cannot kill the soul. Rather, be afraid of the One who can destroy both soul and body in hell."*

Children of Satan are more interested in pleasing man than God. They are more interested in temporal worldly pleasure rather than eternal life with God. Matthew 6:19-21 *"Do not store up for yourselves treasures on earth, where moths and vermin destroy, and where thieves break in and steal. 20 But store up for yourselves treasures in heaven, where moths and vermin do not destroy, and where thieves do not break in and steal. 21 For where your treasure is, there your heart will be also."* The world says to enjoy life because you deserve it or you have earned it. However, all blessings are from God not of your own making. God desires you to store up treasure in heaven that last. If "things" and/or power are you treasure, that is where your heart is. Where do you store your treasure?

Why do Bad Things Happen to Good People?

First of all there are no "good" people in God's eyes as everyone sins. Sin, must be accounted for as God is a "just" God. <u>Romans 6:23</u> *"For the wages of sin is death, but the gift of God is eternal life in Christ Jesus our Lord"* .The good news is that believers will be considered righteous in God's eyes because of Jesus' sacrifice for us!

1. <u>Romans 8:1</u> *"Therefore, there is now no condemnation for those who are in Christ Jesus"* True believers, Christians, will be spared the deserved wrath of God.

2. <u>Ephesians 6:12</u> *"For our struggle is not against flesh and blood, but against the rulers, against the authorities, against the powers of this dark world and against the spiritual forces of evil in the heavenly realms."* God's battle here on earth is not of this world but of the Spiritual World. Many believers are innocent causalities of this spiritual war. They are civilians in the wrong place at the wrong time. However, although they may lose their life here on earth, God has a better place for them in Heaven where there is will be no more sickness or suffering, only pure bliss.

God's View…the "long View" of Creation

No matter what happens to us here on earth, all mankind will live forever. Our life on earth is just a drop in the ocean when compared to eternity. Most of man's time will be spent in Heaven or Hell. Our focus should be on Heaven which is eternal vs. earth which is temporary. Man's "short view" of life focuses on the earth's temporary pleasures which when compared to eternity in Heaven shouldn't even be a consideration.

Christians are to live as aliens here on earth. <u>1 Peter 2:11-12</u> *"Dear friends, I urge you, as foreigners and exiles, to abstain from sinful desires, which wage war against your soul. [12] Live such good lives among the pagans that, though they accuse you of doing wrong, they may see your good deeds and glorify God on the day he visits us."*

Many Americans believe much of what they see on TV or read in the liberal press as true, yet they question clear statements regarding the character of God in the Bible. They dismiss all the factual historical evidence about Jesus. Satan uses the media to mock Christians and create doubt regarding creation and sin's effect on man. Unbelievers, antichrists, are encouraged by what they see and here as they are looking for any excuse to deny the existence of God.

What do You Believe?

What do you believe about creation/evolution? What do you believe about "freewill"? Why does the Bible mention being chosen, appointed, election and predestination 100's of times in the Bible yet freewill is only mentioned 11 times and only in relationship to "freewill offerings"? The 11 myths in the following chapters should correct many misconceptions most people have about God's Word.

Natural man wants to have total control over his/her life. It is much easier to worship a God that he/she creates rather than the God of the Bible. What ever you believe in, you should have facts to support your beliefs. Eternal life in Heaven depends on a personal relationship with Jesus/God. We must flee from sin and search for God's truth. Avoid those who will lead you astray. <u>1 Timothy 4:7-8</u> *"Have nothing to do with godless myths and old wives' tales; rather, train yourself to be godly. [8] For physical training is of some value, but godliness has value for all things, holding promise for both the present life and the life to come."*

Disbelief is Not Forgiven!

If you do not believe that Jesus paid the price for all your sins, then your sins will not be forgiven. Jesus is either your Savior or He will be your judge:

1. John 3:18 *"Whoever believes in him is not condemned, but whoever does not believe stands condemned already because they have not believed in the name of God's one and only Son."*

2. John 3:36 *"Whoever believes in the Son has eternal life, but whoever rejects the Son will not see life, for God's wrath remains on them."* Therefore you will be condemned to spend eternity in Hell created for Satan and his followers.

3. Proverbs 8:17 *"I love those who love me, and those who seek me find me."*

Instead of spending time wondering "why bad things happen to good people", think about why the creator of the universe would care about "sinful me." Psalm 8:4 *"what is man that you are mindful of him, the son of man that you care for him?"* Since life on earth is only a breath or a drop in the ocean compared to eternity, why would God sacrifice His only son to suffer and die for me? A future chapter goes into detail about my questioning why God would save a sinner like me.

Political Correctness

Believing in God is a good start, but even Satan believes in God. Today, it is "politically correct" to believe that God is a loving God and people who do more "good" than "bad" will go to Heaven when they die. In addition, many people think they can "earn" their way into Heaven.. Ephesians 2:8-9 *"For it is by grace you have been saved, through faith—and this is not from yourselves, it is the gift of God — [9] not by works, so that no one can boast."* No one can earn their way into Heaven, it is a gift from God by His unmerited grace..

God is to be worshiped not the world! The "love of the world" comes from Satan not from God. 1st John 2:15-16 *"Do not love the world or anything in the world. If anyone loves the world, the love of the Father is not in him. [16] For everything in the world—the cravings of sinful man, the lust of his eyes and the boasting of what he has and does—comes not from the Father but from the world."* Few people are willing to give up their worldly pleasures and put God 1ˢᵗ in their lives. Therefore, we all fall short of God's desired perfection, which is why we need a savior!

Satan's greatest success in turning people away from God is by appealing to "man's pride. <u>Proverbs 8:13</u> *"I hate pride and arrogance, evil behavior and perverse speech.* <u>Proverbs 16:8</u> *"Pride goes before destruction, a haughty spirit before a fall."* Satan wants man to exalt himself, being "self centered" rather than "God centered". Our pride encourages us to take credit for all that God has blessed us with. Our possessions lead us away from God toward self reliance. Obliviously if all my successes are credited to my hard work or my intelligence, than I don't need God. Satan wants us to think "big me" and "little God". This is just the opposite of God's position in the world.

Think Paradoxically

A paradox is: "a statement or proposition seemingly self-contradictory or absurd but in reality expressing a possible truth." When studying the Bible we should think paradoxically. Several important paradoxes in the Bible are:

1. That "<u>Jesus is 100% God and 100% man</u>". How can any one be more than 100% of anything? Although Jesus' mother was human, Jesus' father was God, the Holy Spirit. <u>Luke 1:34-35</u> *"How will this be," Mary asked the angel, "since I am a virgin?"* ³⁵*The angel answered, "The Holy Spirit will come upon you, and the power of the Most High will overshadow you. So the holy one to be born will be called the Son of God."* <u>Matthew 1:22-23</u> *"All this took place to fulfill what the Lord had said through the prophet:* ²³*"The virgin will be with child and will give birth to a*

son, and they will call him Immanuel" which means, "God with us."

2. <u>Man is both "sinner" and "saint"</u> at the same time. The Bible makes it clear that those who break God's Law, sinners, will experience His wrath. Yet those who believe in the Gospel will receive God's forgiveness and are considered saints. <u>Romans 3:21-24</u> "*But now a righteousness from God, apart from law, has been made known, to which the Law and the Prophets testify. ²²This righteousness from God comes through faith in Jesus Christ to all who believe. There is no difference, ²³for all have sinned and fall short of the glory of God, ²⁴and are justified freely by his grace through the redemption that came by Christ Jesus".* God's law vs. God's grace.

3. <u>The Trinity</u> That God the Father, God the Son and God the Holy Spirit are one in the same person. The word "Trinity" does not appear in the Bible. However, these three dimensions of God's charter are mentioned numerous times throughout the Bible.

Use logic

God gave us a brain and expects us to use it. When our logic is in conflict with God's Word, we are to believe His word, not our logic or the opinions of others as truth.. <u>Isaiah 55:8-9</u> "*For my thoughts are not your thoughts, neither are your ways my ways," declares the LORD."As the heavens are higher than the earth, so are my ways higher than your ways and my thoughts than your thoughts."*

Comparing God's truth to ours limited understanding of the universe would be like comparing a super computer with the brain of a worm. Many rationalities their sins compared to others and believe they will be acceptable to God thinking God grades on a curve. That kind of thinking will lead to their eternal damnation. When in doubt read what God says in His instruction manual, the Bible! Isaiah 16:17 *"Stop trusting in man, who has but a breath in his nostrils. Of what account is he?"* Trust in God not man!

Remember that "God is God and you are not"! Keep an open mind when studying God's Word. God chose flawed people just like us to accomplish His work. Why did God choose Moses a murderer and David a liar, murderer and adulterer? Who are we to question God? Can't the sovereign creator of the universe do as he pleases with his creation?

Enter Through the Narrow Gate

Unfortunately, according to Jesus, only a few people will enter Heaven as most people will follow the pleasures of the world leading to permeant separation from God. Matthew 7:13-14 says, *"Enter through the narrow gate. For wide is the gate and broad is the road that leads to destruction, and many enter through it. ¹⁴But small is the gate and narrow the road that leads to life, and only a few find it."* Faith or belief in Jesus' sacrifice for my sins is the only way into God's Kingdom. Either accept God's gift of forgiveness for all your sins or personally pay the full price all your sins.

John 3:3 *"In reply Jesus declared, "I tell you the truth, no one can see the kingdom of God unless he is born again."* You must be born of the Spirit and become a new creation. How is one born again? It is a gift from God! You can't earn a gift; it is given only to those whom God chooses to give His Spirit to.

Today many people are either too busy or too set in their own self-centered values to search for God's truth. Deuteronomy 6:5 *"Love the Lord your God with all your heart and with all your soul and with all your strength"*. God demands to be number one in our lives, ahead of spouse, children, money, possessions, power or what ever else comes before God in our lives. Most men will be terrified when they meet Jesus and He sends them to Hell. Luke 13:27 *"But he will reply, 'I don't know you or where you come from. Away from me, all you evildoers!'"*

Be a Christian Berean

Paul says that we should be more like the Berean Christians in <u>Acts 17:11</u> *"Now the Bereans were of more noble character than the Thessalonians, for they received the message with great eagerness and examined the Scriptures every day to see if what Paul said was true.* Every Christian should follow Paul's advice and check out scripture to determine fact from fiction. Don't take my word on anything or anyone else for that matter. Open up your Bible and check out these facts for yourself!

CHAPTER 2

THE TRUTH WILL SET YOU FREE

Why me God?

Why does God care about anyone? <u>Hebrews 2:6</u> ***"What is mankind that you are mindful of them, a son of man that you care for him?"*** Why would God save a sinner like me? The Bible says that we all sin and the wages of sin is death. Since we all sin, then everyone deserves God's just judgement. God is omniscient; He knows the future and therefore knows who will accept His mercy and grace. It is only by God's grace that I have come to believe in Him and am considered to be one of His children.

I have no idea why God chose/called me to inherit eternal life:

1. <u>Romans 10:20</u> ***"And Isaiah boldly says, "I was found by those who did not seek me; I revealed myself to those who did not ask for me."***

2. <u>Hebrews 9:15</u> ***"For this reason Christ is the mediator of a new covenant, that those who are called may receive the promised eternal inheritance"*** However, I am extremely

thankful that for some unknown reason, Christ has called me and forgiven me of all my sins!

There certainly is nothing that I have done to deserve salvation. Salvation/eternal life is only offered to those who have faith or belief in Jesus' sacrifice on the cross as payment in full for all our sins. Faith or belief is a gift from God and only understood through the power of His Holy Spirit. The good news about God's gift of grace or His salvation is that it may take place at any time in one's life. For me I was a late bloomer and didn't start seeking God until my mid 40's. I am still growing in faith and have a long way to go. God can even use us in our twilight years. Moses was 80 years old when God called on him to lead His people out of Egypt and into the Promised Land.

Pardoned

The best example of what Christ did for us may be explained in an actual US Government Pardon:

"In 1829 a man named George Wilson was arrested for robbery and murder in a heist of the U.S. mail. He was tried, convicted and sentenced to death by hanging. Some friends intervened on his behalf and were finally able to obtain his pardon from President Andrew Jackson. But when Wilson was informed of his pardon, he refused it, saying he wanted to die.

This left the sheriff with quite a dilemma. How could he execute a man who was officially pardoned? An appeal was made to President Jackson as to what to do. The perplexed president turned the matter over to the U.S. Supreme Court. Chief Justice John Marshall gave this ruling: A pardon is a piece of paper, the value of which depends on its acceptance by the person implicated. Anyone under the sentence of death would hardly be expected to refuse a pardon, but if it is refused, it's no pardon.

Thus George Wilson was executed on the gallows while his signed pardon lay a few hundred feet away on the sheriff's desk!"

The above Government Pardon helps illustrate Jesus' sacrifice or pardon for us and the results if we refuse to accept it. If you reject God's forgiveness of your sins, then, you will die in your sins. John 3:18 *"Whoever believes in him is not condemned, but whoever does not believe stands condemned already because they have not believed in the name of God's one and only Son.*

Why am I Still Alive?

Fortunately I was born in the United States in a small mostly Christine town to Christian parents. I was baptized and confirmed in our local church. Because of my upbringing, I was taught to believe that God created the heavens and earth…that He sent His only son to suffer and die for me. God chose my parents and where I was born. My life would be completely different if I were born and raised in Syria by Moslem parents..

God intervened numerous times in my life in order to get my attention. Psalm 118:18 *"The Lord has chastened me severely, but he has not given me over to death."* There was nothing that I had done to deserve God's saving interventions in my life nor was it my intelligence that led me to choose God. God protected my life over a long period of time before He got my attention. Eventually God got my attention and I started seeking Him in my mid 40's. God drew me into Bible Study where I began to appreciate all that God had done for mankind through His Son's suffering, death and resurrection.

God had to discipline me in order to get my attrition. Psalm 119:71 *"It was good for me to be afflicted so that I might learn your decrees."* Although it took 40+ years to get my attention, God never gave up on me. Even over the previous 20+ years, I have fallen way short of God's commandments, yet He still hasn't abandoned me. Therefore, I am convinced that my Salvation is 100% God and 0% me.

I Did Not Choose God, He Chose Me.

I don't understand why God didn't take my life many years ago. For whatever reason, I am still alive in spite of the many stupid things I have done over my 72 years here on earth. There is nothing that I have done to deserve God's mercy and grace but He has saved my life over and over again ever since my birth.

I was born on a snowy day on January 13, 1945. My parents brought me home to Northeastern Pennsylvania, a town of about 2300 residents. The following headline in the *New York Times* on the day I was born illustrates the difficult but victorious times in my life.

"3D FLEETPLANES SINK 25 JAPANESE SHIPS,
HIT 13 MORE IN CONVOYS OFF INDO-CHINA;
GERMAN BULGE IN BELGIUM IS COLLAPSING"

This headline illustrates difficult but victorious times in my life.

My 1st Brush With Death

I first began to be aware of life in 1st grade and remember Mrs. Stone my 1st grade teacher. Soon after stating 2nd grade, I was hit with a stone in my right eye. I didn't tell my parents because this occurred as a result from a stone throwing fight with several older boys. The next day, my mother found me sleeping in my clothes closet because the sun light hurt my eyes and I was very sleepy. My mother took me to our local eye doctor who imminently called a neurologist in Binghamton, New York. I was rushed to their hospital and operated on immediately due to a blood clot on my brain.

If I hadn't had that operation within hours I would not be writing this today. The pressure was relieved from my brain by going through my right eye. They were more concerned in saving my life than worrying about my sight. After I was out of danger, my doctors didn't think I would ever see out of my right eye. In addition, the doctors feared that the infection in my right eye could spread to my lift eye, leaving me totally blind. I even remember overhearing a doctor telling my parents about a fitting me for a glass eye.

Everyone was relieved when penicillin, a new drug prevented my eye infection from spreading to my left eye. I spent several weeks in the hospital and the rest of the year at home recovering. I had to repeat the 2nd grade due to my accident.

About a year later I began to see light through my right eye and over time I was able to have corrected vision of 20/30. To date I have 20/20 corrected vision in my left eye. My right eye is permanently dilated with limited vision but I still see 20/20 overall. God's angles were certainly looking after me. <u>Hebrews 1:14</u> ***"Are not all angels ministering spirits sent to serve those who will inherit salvation?"***

Why Not Viet Nam?

Not only was God watching out for me when I was 6 years old but continued after my senior year in high school. My fathers company went out of business so my parents couldn't afford to send me to college. I planned on going into the Air Force where they would pay for my college under their "operation boot strap" program. In the last phase of my physical exam, the eye doctor asked about my dilated pupil in my right eye even though I passed the vision exam. I was given a 1-Y deferment due to the fact that my right eye wasn't sensitive to light. This meant that I wasn't qualified for military service unless of a major war.

I was very disappointed that I couldn't join the Air Force and I ended up working in an automotive retail store at home. There I was able to help my family by paying their mortgage on our home until my dad could find a new job. After several months I was promoted to assistant manager. Concerns over Vietnam were escalating and the military draft became a necessary way of life for all males after finishing high school. You could receive a deferment if you were going to college. At least I knew I wouldn't be drafted and could continue a career without having the draft interfere with my life.

Several months after I was settled in my new job I was approached by a Marine Recruiter who was aware of my desire to join the military. He told me that the Marines were willing to overlook my eye defect and allow me to join the Marines. Had he approached me soon after my being turned down by the Air Force, I would have jumped at the opportunity to join the any military branch that would give me the opportunity to earn a college degree.

Had I joined the Marines, I would have been in Vietnam during the Teat Offence where several thousand marines were killed. Not only did I avoid the war but I was able to pay the mortgage on my parent's home for 3 years until my dad could afford to take it over.

I Am no Saint

Don't get the impression that I was some sort of Saint. I did love my parents but I also gave them many gray hairs. The New York state line was a little over 11 miles from my Pennsylvania home and the legal drinking age was 18. At 16 I was drinking in bars in New York state and God's angles must have helped me arrive home safely on many occasions. Once I drove to a local NY bar, consumed 10 draft beers and made it home in 1 hour. I couldn't count the number of total car wrecks that I survived over my youth. There is no question in my mind that God has been looking after me even though I resisted His call for many years.

My 2ⁿᵈ Brush With Death

The 2nd serious accident occurred after I graduated from college. I was driving from Corning New York to Penn State University with a girl friend. We had been drinking and it was late at night and snowing very hard. I missed a curve in the road and plowed onto the guard rail. The steering wheel shaft pierced the seat head rest where I was sitting and the transmission was pushed up level with the front seat. Luckily I was thrown to the passenger side of the car preventing me from being skewered by the steering wheel shaft. However the transmission shattered my right arm and gave me a concussion. My girl friend actually saved my life. Even though she had a broken back she set me upright preventing me from choking on my own blood. The girl ended up in a body cast for over a month and I still have screws and wire in my right arm.

My First Marriage Was a Disaster

Although my 1st marriage produced two wonderful children, God humbled me in many ways. My x-wife had a severe spending problem that cost us our marriage, caused me to take another job in another state, put me in serious debt and almost cost me the loss of my two children.

One day I found out that my wife created over $70,000 in bank and credit card debt plus cleaning out all our savings and investments. She rented a post office box so I never saw the mail therefore had no idea of our debt. I didn't find out until I got a call from a creditor which exposed her deception. She had claimed things were wedding gifts or gifts from her parents who were very poor.

At first she agreed to marriage counseling but later refused any help. I accepted a new job in another state which I thought would give us a fresh start. Although our finances would be extremely tight for many years, we could have survived.

The final straw came several months after we moved into a home purchased for us by my new employer. When I returned home from a business trip, I walked into our living room with all brand new furniture and accessories. My wife told me that her grandfather paid for everything and had receipts marked "paid". I knew her grandfather didn't have that kind of money so I called the furniture store. The store informed me that my wife had bought everything on credit. We still were trying to sell our home in New York, were in debt up to our eyebrows and would have to pay my company loan on our current home once our home in New York State sold.

I gave my wife an ultimatum; she was to choose a marriage counselor, lawyer, pastor or financial advisor. She would have to agree to financial counseling if anyone she selected would suggest she needed the counselling after exposing our entire financial situation. However she refused counselling under any circumstances. I told her that she left me no choice but to to file for divorce.

I couldn't use my company's attorneys as my wife had talked to them so they couldn't represent either of us. Therefore, I had to find an attorney on my own. The next day I took off work and to talk to an attorney. My wife called me late in the afternoon to see what I had done. I told her that I hired an attorney and she was welcome to use him' My wife claimed that she was at the grocery store and we could discuss the matter when she came home.

My wife and two children never came home. I called her mother and everyone I could think of to find out where my children were. My oldest son was 3 years old and my daughter was 1 year old. I didn't know where they were for over a month. Finally the local lawyer I hired called me telling that he had some good news and some bad news for me. The good news was that he was finally was able to serve my wife with divorce papers. The bad news was that my wife flew into town, had a moving van there and cleaned out our home of everything in our home while I was out of town on business.

I came home to an empty house, sat on the floor and began to cry and laugh at the same time. She had my children, cleaned out all my savings, left me with over $70,000.00 in debt and now had all my possessions. She even charged me with her and a boy friend's air fare plus the moving company's expenses to me after she cleaned out the house.

The next couple of years were difficult to say the least. However, several years I married a great woman and we have been married for over 37 years. Eventually, I received full custody of my 2 children when I found out she basically abandoned them to be raised by two alcoholic women. My wife has raised them since they were 4 and 6 years old and as far as they are concerned, she is their real Mom..

After 4 miscarriages we had our first girl together and two years later we had a son. We are very blessed with 4 great adult children and 4 grandchildren. Both our girls are married and both boys are employed. Without trusting in God, I could not have made it through all the above. God disciplines His children which makes us stronger by depending on Him.

My 3ʳᵈ Brush With Death

Another miracle occurred several years later when my wife, two children and I were returning home to Huntington, WV form Richmond VA. We were traveling on a two lane steep winding road with a mountain on one side and a several hundred foot drop off on the other side of the road. The first thing I saw after coming around the sharp curve. Was a tractor trailer coming up the hill passing another tractor trailer in my lane. I remember saying to my wife, "my God he is in my lane". My son was sleeping up on the back ledge above the back seat and my daughter was sleeping on the back seat.

We glanced off the tractor trailer and were slammed into the mountain side of the road after impact. Again, God's angle was looking out for us as my son was thrown onto the back seat on top of his sister. The back window was shattered and the back roof of the car was level with the ledge where my son was sleeping. Had he been seated in the proper place in the back seat with a seat belt on, he would have been killed.

He only suffered a scrape on his back from the roof collapsing on him when he was thrown onto the back seat. However, we didn't find this out until he was rushed in an ambulance to the nearest hospital on a stiff board and a neck brace. A x-rayed showed no neck or back injury. We never did see our car again because a friend picked up our luggage and personal belongings from the junk yard where they had towed our car. Witnesses who saw the condition of the car couldn't believe that anyone could have lived through that accident.

I Am a "High Bottom Alcoholic"

As mentioned earlier, I began drinking in bars at the age of 16. For many years I was able to drink most people under the table. I had convinced myself that I wasn't an alcoholic because I never drank in the morning. However, as I grew older I was drinking more on weekends and remembering it less. I was not a mean drunk which prolonged other's potential criticism about my excessive drinking. Drinking on weekends and getting drunk was becoming more frequent.

One summer Sunday afternoon my, my wife and our two younger children were watching TV in our family room. I believe the year was 1994. While sitting in my chair and drinking, I think my 3rd screwdriver, I complained to God as to why my life was so difficult; Our two oldest children were in out- of- state universities which we could not afford, I was self employed and we were having a difficult time making ends meet.

My prayer to God was for Him to bless my three business that I was running so I could continue to live a life style that I couldn't afford. God gave me a clear answer, "stop drinking"! I told my wife that I was not going to drink any more. She didn't believe me at but I have not had a drink for over 23 years. God took away my desire to drink. A recovering alcoholic later told me that I was a "high bottom drunk" because I bottomed out at the top rather after I had lost everything.

God intervened in my life and got me involver is a serious non denominational Bible study, BSF, Bible Study Fellowship. After my 1st year I was invited into leadership and several years later I helped teach their new children's program for 7 years. I left BSF after 9 years and have rejoined BSF as a student about 8 years ago. Who can resist God's will?

My Most Resent Near Death Experience

My most recent near death accident occurred on July 14, 2007 when I fell 35 feet to the ground while cutting down a tree in our back yard. (Only about 20% survive from a fall from such a distance). However, I shattered my left ankle, my left hip was mush, I broke my pelvis in half, fractured my right pelvis, broke 3 ribs and punctured my lung. I spent over two and a half months in the hospital plus many months in rehab. A year later I had a complete hip and socket replacement. Today I am able to walk without a cane and live a normal life.

Is all the above just good luck that I wasn't killed or at least crippled? What are the odds of that? I believe my time which is determined by God has not come yet. For some reason God must want me around for a while.

God Turned Disaster into a Blessing

Not only has God saved me physically numerous times, God also saved my family from financial ruin. I was self-employed and running three different companies. In addition, we were living beyond our means and "robbing Peter to pay Paul" using credit card debt to supplement our income shortages. As our debt continued to mount, my prayer was that God would bless my three businesses so we could continue our current life style and help us get out of debt. However, my accident accelerated our debt problem into a debt crisis. In order to survive, we borrowed money from every credit card company that would give us credit. At that time we still had good credit. I was unable to work but I could not receive any unemployment compensation because I was self-employed.

God had a different, "get out of debt plan" plan which was painful at first but turned out to be in our best interest. We had no choice but to not only walk away from our home of 24 years but also forced to declare bankruptcy.

Today, we are totally out of debt thanks to a good friend from church who loaned us money to buy a home that we could afford. I doubt we could have been able to even rent a decent home for my family with our damaged credit. No bank would touch us due to our bankruptcy and home foreclosure. The good news was I was eligible to collect Social Security with back benefits because of my age. We are also blessed with two girls married and two boys employed.

We love our home and were able to paid off our friend's loan five years ago and refinance our home at very low rate. Now with the exception of our low mortgage payment and car payments, we are completely debt free.

You can't imagine the burden that has been lifted off my wife and family. God does answer prayer but not necessarily in the manner we expect. Today, God has blessed me physically, financially and spiritually!

God's Mercy and Grace

The whole point of this chapter was to illustrate God's mercy and grace for a sinner like me. There is a lot of dirty laundry that I failed to mention and nothing that I have done to deserve any of God's protection. I have no idea why I am so blessed.

God has taken me kicking and screaming into faith after about of 45 years of rebellion. I have been actively studying the bible for over 20 years and been involved in many different bible studies which continues to strengthened my faith. I am still a sinner today but I do repent and give thanks for Jesus' payment for my sins. The closer I come to God, the more I recognize my sinfulness. Could it be that God wanted the truth about Him to be published in this book?

CHAPTER 3

································

THE TRUTH WILL SET YOU FREE

Myth #1: Evolution…A Scientific Fact!

Is Man the Product of Chance Over Time?

Are we a product of chance, "evolution", over time or was there a creator involved in the creation? Atheist and the "never God" people believe that man evolved from chemical reactions occurring over billions of years; In essence they worship "The God of Chance". God's magnificent creation is visible to everyone to see and marvel over its beauty and complexity. Psalm 19:1-2 ***"The heavens declare the glory of God; the skies proclaim the work of his hands.² Day after day they pour forth speech; night after night they reveal knowledge."***

Man will not be excused for giving credit for His creation to someone or something else. Romans 1:20 ***"For since the creation of the world God's invisible qualities—his eternal power and divine nature—have been clearly seen, being understood from what has been made, so that people are without excuse."*** Believers in evolution actually are denying the existence of God therefore are condemned and will justly suffer His wrath eternally.

Scientific Fact vs. Scientific Theory

Believers in evolution are "Never God Elites" who will do anything to convince others regarding their belief in creation. They feel comforted by getting as many people as possible to believe in the same lie about evolution. Unfortunately they have been successful and control the majority of our media, Hollywood, most of universities and politics. They want everyone to believe that creation is only an outdated religious fable.

In order to believe in evolution, people must deny basic science and math. Until a scientific theory can be considered to be scientific fact, it must be able to be duplicated and observed by measurable results. Until then, it remains scientific theory.

All evolutionary theories fail to explain:

1. What started the evolutionary process? The "big "bang theory" falls as it doesn't explain what caused the big bang in the first place.

2. What caused the first living cell to form and then divide? Never has anyone been able to create a living cell out on inert matter and have it duplicate or divide into more complex cells.

3. What came first the chicken or the egg? In order for a chicken to exist there must be a female chicken and a male rooster to produce a fertilized egg. This holds true for all mammals and most other species.

Creationists agree that some evolving within a species takes place over time through natural selection, .i.e. over time i.e. bigger, taller, stronger etc. However they find no evidence of one species ever mutating into another species. Fruit flies have a very short life cycle and have been studied intently for decades. Fruit flies have been subjected to s experiments that simulate early earth in order to prove that mutations could produce a new or different spice. Through billions of experiments over many decades, the only mutations exhibited were various stages of deformity.

Evolutionists Are Bad at Math

To believe in evolution evolving form nothing into microorganisms and way down the road, into complex man, one must allow for extensive long periods of time. Evolutionist must use billions and billions of years to order to make their theory of evolution remotely believable.

Evolutionists also suggest that because there are billions or trillions of planets in our solar system, therefore life must exist somewhere else out there also. The truth is that no matter how many planets there are in our universe someone or something had to cause their existence. They use the same logic for creation on earth. If earth is old enough eventually life will form and evolve.

Evolutionists, never God elites, have convinced much of the world that evolution has occurred over these extended periods of time. They deny there is a God/creator. Since there is no God there is no judgement or Hell. If they are wrong, they will be extremely unhappy eternally. Their short lived pleasures in this sinful world will be soon forgotten with billions and billions of years spent separated from God forever. The big problem with their math is that: <u>One billion times zero still equals zero!</u>

The Bible is very clear about creation. Just as a building needs a builder, creation needs a creator and that creator is The God of the Universe. <u>Genesis 1:1</u> ***"In the beginning God created the heavens and the earth.*** There is no evidence of one species ever mutating in to another species. The reason the "Never God Elites" don't comprehend God's creation is That God knows they are not His children blinds them to the truth! <u>2 Corinthians 4:3-4</u> ***"And even if our gospel is veiled, it is veiled to those who are perishing. [4] The god of this age has blinded the minds of unbelievers, so that they cannot see the light of the gospel that displays the glory of Christ, who is the image of God."***

All unbelievers will experience eternal suffering where they will never die. How would you feel if you invented the greatest machine ever imagined or miracle drug that cured every disease and some dishonest person took credit for it? God is not pleased with those who lie about His creation. Proverbs 12:22: *"The Lord detests lying lips, but delights in men who are truthful."*

Flat Earth Belief

Hundreds of years ago man believed that the earth was flat and if one got too close to the end of the earth that you could fall off into space. Man also believed at one time that the earth was the center of the universe and the sun and all the planets revolved around earth. These paradigms took many years to change before people finally believed the truth that earth was actually round and that it rotated around the sun. The one thing people didn't question was how the universe and man came into existence. Most western civilized countries believed that a "supreme being" or a God created the heavens, earth and man.

That paradigm took a major shift after Charles Darwin published his book, "The Origin of Species". Darwin witnessed in his visit to different parts of the world, that many different species had similar features. After intensive research, he concluded that life on earth evolved over millions rather than through a divine creator. This gained scientific approval over time until it became the "law of the land" here in the United States. Today, all public schools and most secular universities teach evolution as a scientific fact.

At first evolution was just taught as an alternate theory to creation. As more and more secularists fought to teach this theory, they became the denominate voice and made great gains in the scientist community and also in the secular media. Eventually the evolutionists won the battle and today creation isn't even allowed to be taught in public schools and universities as an alternative theory to evolution. This is also what many scientists and educators today demand you to believe! At best evolution is a theory but by no means a scientific fact! The truth about Darwin's evolution theory is that there is no scientific evidence to support this theory! The only truth regarding the evolution theory is that it *cannot* be proven scientifically!

A noted astrophysicist, Sir Fred Hoyle, stated that chance process could not have formed the biochemical machinery of the cell, especially the enzymes. A famous quote from Hoyle: *"Belief in the chemical evolution of the first cell from lifeless chemicals is equivalent to believing that a tornado could sweep through a junkyard and form a functional Boeing 747."*

The Alabama Textbook Disclaimer

The majority of states don't allow creation to be taught even though there is no scientific evidence proving that macro evolution, evolution from one species into another species, has ever occurred.

on Alabama in an exception and mentions creation in their text books:

"A *message from the Alabama State Board of Education:*

This textbook discusses evolution, a controversial theory some scientists present as a scientific explanation for the origin of living things, such as plants, animals, and humans. No one was present when life first appeared on earth. Therefore, any statement about life's origin should be considered as theory, not fact.

The word "evolution" may refer to many types of change. Evolution describes changes that occur within a species. (White moths, for example, may "evolve" into gray moths.) This process is microevolution, which can be observed and described as fact. Evolution may also refer to the change of one living thing to another, such as reptiles into birds. This process, called macroevolution, has never been observed and should be considered a theory. Evolution also refers to the unproven belief that random, undirected forces produced a world of living things.

There are many unanswered questions about the origin of life which are not mentioned in your textbook, including:

1. *Why did the major groups of animals suddenly appear in the fossil record (known as the "Cambrian Explosion")?*

2. *Why have no new major groups of living things appeared in the fossil record for a long time?*

3. *Why do major groups of plants and animals have no transitional forms in the fossil record?*

4. *How did you and all living things come to possess such a complete and complex set of "Instructions" for building a living body?*

Study hard and keep an open mind. Some day you may contribute to the theory of how living things appeared earth."

Is There a God?

In spite of the controversial evidence, biology students are taught today that man came into being through evolution over billions of years and is proven through scientific research, observation and carbon dating. If everything on earth came into being by chance or evolution, then there is no God and all religions that believe that there is a God are nothing but a lie and believers are to be pitied for their ignorance.

Satan's greatest weapon against belief in God is to convince people that He doesn't exist. "Darwinian evolution" gives atheists, Never God deniers cover for their anti-God belief. The majority of these scientists do not want to entertain any theory which includes a creator or intelligent design.

A Gallop poll showed that strict Darwinism is held by only 9% of the general population where as a special poll of biologist in the National Academy of Science showed that 95% say they do not believe in God. Is there any bias seen here?

Isn't pure science supposed to test and question possible alternative solutions as to how man came into being rather than intimidate scientists with opposing views? Scientists who believe there is no God state evolution as "fact" when evolution is impossible to be proven scientifically?

The main stream news media has an agenda which is anti-Christian and fail to report any facts that don't fit into their atheistic bias. However, they are anxious to report in great detail stories that picture Christians in a negative light.

How Old is Earth?

In order for evolution to have any credibility, the earth must be billions and billions of years old. Scientists claim the earth to be about 4.56 billion years old and the universe to be about 14 billion years old. There is no way a "young earth" could support evolutionary theory.

The earth's age is based on the radioisotope dating of rocks and meteorites, a technique developed during the last century. Age estimates for the rest of the universe follow largely from the big-bang theory. These multi-billion year time spans are sometimes called deep time, corresponding to deep space.

Evolutionary models for life, earth, and space are questioned today by a significant group of scientists worldwide. These scientists were skeptical of the evolutionary time scale which dominates modern geology. An excellent review of their work is written in their book: THOUSANDS...NOT BILLIONS by Dr. Don DeYoung.

They reviewed the assumptions and procedures used in estimation the age of rock strata and they recognized multiple weaknesses. This group identifies itself with the acronym RATE which stands for Radioisotopes and the Age of The Earth. The "seven RATE" scientists include two geologists (Steven Austin, Andrew Snelling) a geophysicist (John Baumgardner), three physicists (Eugene Chaffin, Don DeYoung, Russell Humphreys), and a meteorologist (Larry Vardiman, chairman of RATE). Steve Boyd, a biblical Hebrew scholar, also joined the RATE effort. Each of the team members holds an earned doctorate.

One principle agreed on by all the RATE members is that the earth is young, on the order of 6,000 years old. Following are some of the major results of their findings:

1. *For some years there has been a growing realization that carbon-14 atoms are found where they are not expected.* With a half-life of 5,730 years, C-14 should no longer exist within "ancient" fossils, carbonate rocks, or coal. Yet small quantities of C-14 are indeed found in such samples on a worldwide scale.

2. *.Zircons play a prominent part in the RATE studies.* These are tiny crystals which often occur in granite, one of the most abundant rock types on earth. Within their crystal structures, many zircons hold helium atoms which result from the decay of internal uranium atoms. RATE research obtained some of the first high-precision data on helium diffusion in zircon. A theoretical model based on this data gives an age for the earth of about 6,000 years. The presence of helium in zircons is a serious challenge to the concept of deep time. The helium also represents compelling evidence of accelerated nuclear decay in the past.

3. *Radiohalos are tiny spherical defects in rocks.* They result from the decay of clusters of radioactive atoms, mainly uranium and polonium. The frequent occurrence of these halos in rocks is evidence for widespread nuclear decay. Halos are present in abundance in granites whose formation accompanied the Genesis flood. This indicates that a large-scale acceleration of nuclear decay occurred during the year-long Flood event.

4. *Many rock units worldwide were analyzed by radioisotope dating techniques.* Some examples of concordance, or agreement in age were found, while many other examples showed discordance, or disagreement. In fact, both extremes often occurred for the same rock unit. The RATE results raise serious cautions concerning the interpretation of

isochrons. The conclusion is that no isochron age can be trusted with confidence.

5. ***The concept of accelerated decay arises many times in the RATE work.*** It is the   logical inference of placing millions or billions of year's worth of nuclear decay, at present rates, into a short time frame. The episodes of increased nuclear activity appear to have occurred during the creation week and also during the flood of Noah's day. The evidence of vast amounts of decay include the abundance of nuclear decay products, high concentrations of helium atoms residing in zircon crystals, radiohalos, and fission tracks.

For a detailed analysis on the age of the earth, please read Dr. DeYoung's book, *THOUSANDS…NOT BILLIONS* crystals, radiohalos, and fission tracks.

Intelligent Design

Although the evolutionary theory is largely believed today, some scientists are viewing the scientific evidence of evolution with more and more skepticism. The discovery of complex DNA has caused some to acknowledge that a supreme being may have starting the creative process. The conclusion they use to explain all the inconsistencies in evolution is "intelligent design". Following are some of the key people and their arguments against evolution who challenged the Darwin entrenched natural selection paradigm:

1. **Michael Denton**

Michael Denton, a Ph.D. in biochemistry wrote, *"Evolution: A Theory in Crisis"* published in 1986 which started a serious debate about Darwin's evolutionary theory. Denton agreed that microevolution was plausible but that the macro evolutionary evidence had very little empirical support. ***"Macroevolution-continuous evolutionary development through the selection of random mutations-is not supported by*** *findings in any area of biology. The theory is supported neither by empirical evidence nor by thought experiments, that is, by attempts at reconstructing plausible evolutionary pathways."* He was convinced of the complexity of nature. *"The multifunctionality of things…struck me as an extraordinary thing to experience, and this level of complexity was not easily reducible to a simple, continuous, random process."* Denton concluded in his book:

"One might have expected that a theory of such cardinal importance, a theory that literally changed the world, would have been something more than metaphysical, something more than a myth.

Ultimately the Darwinian theory of evolution is no mere nor less than the great cosmogenic myth of the twentieth century…In the final analysis we still know very little about how new forms of life arise."

2. Philip Johnson

Phillip Johnson, Berkeley law professor, was inspired by Denton book and published his own book: "Darwin on Trial" in 1991. Johnson spoke at many universities and wrote six books questioning evolution as anything other than theory. In all his books Johnson states *"that every area of relevant scientific evidence tends to falsify Darwinism rather than confirm it."*

As an attorney, Johnson wanted to get rid of all biases in to relationship to both creation and evolution. In his many debates with Darwin evolutionists, Johnson was able to uncover strong atheist biased as anything theory's related to God or not as a direct result of science were rejected outright! The intellectuals don't want to be confused with facts i.e. "the fossil record records which fail to show one single transition from one species to another".

Johnson was quoted as saying *"Most people in the intellectual world are certain that evolution must be true because it is the only tenable naturalistic explanation for the development of complex life, or life in general, and it therefore must be true if non-naturalistic explanations such as creation are ruled ineligible for consideration. The evidence is built up upon this pre-existing theoretical certainty based on philosophical presupposition. Non-evolutionary explanations of the evidence are not considered, and therefore the evidentiary support which seems to exist is the product of the cultural certainty rather than its cause of support."*

3. Michael Behe

The next important scientist on the scene to debate evolution was Michael Behe, a Lehigh University biochemist. He argued in the <u>New York Times</u> stating that: "intelligent design theory" does a far better job of explaining the origin of complex biochemical machines within the cell than does Darwinian Theory. In August 1996 he published: <u>"Darwin's Black Box"</u> which stressed the "irreducible complexity" of nature.

The *New York Times* summarized Behe's argument that *"many of the biochemical machines inside the cell, such as the tiny outboard motor called the flagellum, exhibited an eerie kind of complexity that defied Darwinian explanations. These systems, said Behe, could not function if any one part were removed; they were "irreducibly complex."* The *Times* goes on to say *that such complexity presents us with "an overwhelming argument for "intelligent design".*

Behe used a quote in Darwin's book, <u>The Origin of the Species</u>; to make his point about "irreducible complexity". *"If it could be demonstrated that any complex organ existed which could not possibly have been formed by numerous, successive, slight modifications, my theory would absolutely break down."* Then Behe goes on to say *"the truth is that sub cellular organisms are extremely complex and scientists have no idea how these systems could have evolved step-by- Darwinian-step."*

4. William Dembski

William Dembski holds a PhD in mathematics and philosophy and is a research professor at Baylor University. *"Demski gave credibility to "intelligent design" through his mathematic filter formula. The filter took the form of a three-tier system of conceptual sieves, linked with a step-by-step procedure that Dembski claimed could positively identify the action of intelligent design in any system or phenomenon in nature. He argued that the filter is analytically "robust" That is, it can be shown as highly precise and reliable and can be applied to many different fields of research. The filter has become the most important procedural plank of a putative new paradigm that is "geared to the detection of design" in biological systems."*

In spite of all the scientific evidence mentioned above, the main line media and most educators won't allow creation to be mentioned as possible answer to where actually man came from.

Belief in Evolution is Disbelief in God

What you believe in will determine where you will spend eternity. Obviously if you don't believe that God created the Heavens and earth than you won't believe in the accuracy of the Bible. Many former Bible skeptics like C. S. Lewis and Josh McDowell, after researching the Bible's accuracy have been converted to Christianity. In every instance, historical locations and people quoted in the Bible have proven to be true through archaeology and other ancient manuscripts. Prophecies given hundreds of years prior to their fulfillment have come to pass.

Every chapter in the Old Testament alludes to the coming Messiah, savior or redeemer. The Jews of the Old Testament were looking for a conquering king who would restore the nation of Israel to its former stature under King David. However, God's redemptive plan was to send His son, the "suffering servant" to pay the penalty for man's sins. God's love for man offered a way out from the cycle of death and decay after Adam's disobedience. Genesis 2:17 *"but you must not eat from the tree of the knowledge of good and evil, for when you eat from it you will certainly die."*

Someday Jesus will return and reign as the "King of Kings and "Lord of Lords" over the entire world. Then every knee will bow and recognize Jesus as the true God. Isaiah 45:23 *"Before me every knee will bow by me every tongue will swear."* Romans 14:11 *"'It is written: "As surely as I live,' says the Lord, 'every knee will bow before me; every tongue will acknowledge God.'"* At Jesus' second coming, He will judge the world and separate believers from unbelievers.

The Bible Proves Creation Through Prophecy

Throughout the Bible God fore told future events that came true hundreds of years later. God told Abraham that his descendants would be slaves in Egypt for 400 years. Joseph, who was betrayed by his brothers later saved the Israelites from starvation and was a hero in Egypt for many years. Years later the Egyptians forgot how Joseph had saved their people from starvation. God had blessed the Israelites with many children and the Egyptians became fearful that they could revolt and take over their country. Four hundred years later Moses freed them, leading them to the "Promised Land". Instead of being grateful of their freedom, the people grumbled and doubted God. Because of their disbelief, they had to wander in the desert for 40 years until all who disbelieved died out in the desert. Their children finally were allowed to enter the Promised Land.

God's chosen people, the Jews/Israelites, continually rebelled against God. After finally entering in the Promised land, they demanded a King rather than relying on God. God relented and things went downhill from then on. Israel had a few good Kings but mostly were evil Kings. They worshiped false gods so God removed them form their land. The Northern part of the country was exiled to Assyria and later Jerusalem and the Southern part of the country was exiled to Babylon.

Isaiah Foretold of the Jews Return to Israel

Isaiah, one of the Old Testaments Major Prophets foretold that the fall of Jerusalem would not occur by the Assyrians who previously had conquered the Northern Kingdom of Israel. Jerusalem was under siege and ready to be overthrown by the Assyrians but at the last minute God sent an angle that destroyed 185,000 of their army and the remaining army retreated back to Assyria. Because of Judah's continued idol worship, God had them exiled by the Babylonians.

First God used the Assyrians to punish the Jews in the Northern Kingdom of Israel then God used the Babylonians to punish the Jews and the Assyrians in the Southern Kingdom. The Babylonians defeated the Assyrians and conquered Israel's Southern Kingdom.

Next God used the Persians to punish the Babylonians from their cruel treatment of the Jews in while in their captivity. After this God's wrath toward the Jews was complete and he sough to comfort them by returning them back to the land God promised them through Abraham and the prophets.

Isaiah not only predicted all this would happen but also the name of the king who would release the Jews from their exile and return them to Jerusalem to rebuild the Jewish temple. Isaiah correctly named King Cyrus 100 years before he was born. Isaiah 44:28 *"who says of Cyrus, 'He is my shepherd and will accomplish all that I please; he will say of Jerusalem, "Let it be rebuilt," and of the temple, "Let its foundations be laid."* Isaiah 45:13 *"I will raise up Cyrus] in my righteousness: I will make all his ways straight. He will rebuild my city and set my exiles free, but not for a price or reward, says the LORD Almighty."*

Isaiah Foretold of Jesus, "The Suffering Servant"

Over 700 years before Jesus was born, Isaiah made the following predictions about Jesus, God's "suffering servant". Isaiah 53:3-12 *"He was despised and rejected by mankind, a man of suffering, and familiar with pain. Like one from whom people hide their faces he was despised, and we held him in low esteem.*[4] *Surely he took up our pain and bore our suffering, yet we considered him punished by God, stricken by him, and afflicted.* [5] *But he was pierced for our transgressions, he was crushed for our iniquities; the punishment that brought us peace was on him, and by his wounds we are healed.* [6] *We all, like sheep, have gone astray, each of us has turned to our own way; and the LORD has laid on him the iniquity of us all.* [7] *He was oppressed and afflicted, yet he did not open his mouth; he was led like a lamb to the slaughter, and as a sheep before its shearers is silent, so he did not open his mouth.* [8] *By oppression and judgment he was taken away. Yet who of his generation protested? For he was cut off from the land of the living; for the transgression of my people he was punished.* [9] *He was assigned a grave with the wicked, and with the rich in his death, though he had done no violence, nor was any deceit in his mouth.* [10] *Yet it was the LORD's will to crush him and cause him to suffer, and though the LORD makes his life an offering for sin, he will see his offspring and prolong his days, and the will of the LORD will prosper in his hand.* [11]*After he has suffered, he will see the light of life and be satisfied; by his knowledge my righteous servant will justify many, and he will bear their iniquities.* [12] *Therefore I will give him a portion among the great, and he will divide the spoils with the strong because he poured out his life unto death, and was numbered with the transgressors. For he bore the sin of many, and made intercession for the transgressors.*

Isaiah even predicted that God would send His Son, mighty God, and He would reign forever Isaiah 9:6-7 *"For to us a child is born, to us a son is given, and the government will be on his shoulders. And he will be called Wonderful Counselor, Mighty God, Everlasting Father, Prince of Peace.* [7] *Of the greatness of his government and peace there will be no end. He will reign on David's throne and over his kingdom, establishing and upholding it with justice and righteousness from that time on and forever. The zeal of the LORD*

Almighty will accomplish this." Jesus is the Son of God, the King of Kings and Lord of Lords.

The above prophesies about Jesus during His life took place about 700 years before He was born. God's prophet, Isaiah, couldn't have been more accurate than if it were written after Jesus' time on earth. Isaiah also prophesied: Isaiah 7:14 *"Therefore the Lord himself will give you a sign: The virgin will conceive and give birth to a son, and will call him Immanuel."* Immanuel means "God with us". Jesus was "God in the flesh", God living among His chosen people. The Virgin Mary, the mother of Jesus had the Holy Spirit as His biological father. Jesus was despised, suffered, pierced, silent, was crucified between two criminals yet buried in a rich man's tomb. What are the odds of all these prophecies just being lucky guesses by Isaiah?

Three hundred years earlier or about 1000 years before the birth of Jesus, King David also talked about Jesus' suffering in Psalm 22. Do any for the following words sound familiar? Psalm 22:1 *"My God, my God, why have you forsaken me? Why are you so far from saving me, so far from my cries of anguish"?* These were the same words Jesus spoke on the cross just before He gave up His life. Psalm 22:6-8 *"But I am a worm and not a man, scorned by everyone, despised by the people.* [7] *All who see me mock me; they hurl insults, shaking their heads.* [8] *"He trusts in the LORD," they say, "let the LORD rescue him. Let him deliver him, since he delights in him."* Psalm 22:14-18 *"I am poured out like water, and all my bones are out of joint. My heart has turned to wax; it has melted within me.* [15] *My mouth is dried up like a potsherd, and my tongue sticks to the roof of my mouth; you lay me in the dust of death.* [16] *Dogs surround me, a pack of villains encircles me; they pierce my hands and my feet.* [17] *All my bones are on display; people stare and gloat over me.* [18] *They divide my clothes among them and cast lots for my garment."* All this happpened at Jesus' crucification although prophesied 1000 years earlier.

To question the accuracy of the Bible one must discount the enormous odds against the probability of all these events which were accurately written hundreds of years before they actually took place. To me this alone validates that man is a product of God, not evolution.

Children of the Devil will never accept the God or the truth in God's Word. It is foolishness to those who are perishing. 2 Thessalonians 2:9-12 *"The coming of the lawless one will be in accordance with how Satan works. He will use all sorts of displays of power through signs and wonders that serve the lie,* [10] *and all the ways that wickedness deceives those who are perishing. They perish because they refused to love the truth and so be saved.* [11] *For this reason God sends them a powerful delusion so that they will believe the lie* [12] *and so that all will be condemned who have not believed the truth but have delighted in wickedness.* However, God's children will eventually seek and find Him on His timetable not ours.

What you Believe Has Eternal Consequences

There are still many questions relating to the creation of man and the universe. Science has not been able to prove or disprove the existence of God. It takes faith to believe in the "God of Chance" just as it takes faith to believe in the God of the Bible. Faith is not something you can prove. Hebrews 11:6 *"And without faith it is impossible to please God, because anyone who comes to him must believe that he exists and that he rewards those who earnestly seek him."* Denying the existence of God does have eternal consequences. Hebrews 10:29-31 *"How much more severely do you think someone deserves to be punished who has trampled the Son of God underfoot, who has treated as an unholy thing the blood of the covenant that sanctified them, and who has insulted the Spirit of grace?* [30] *For we know him who said, "It is mine to avenge; I will repay." and again, "The Lord will judge his people."* [31] *It is a dreadful thing to fall into the hands of the living God."*

Conclusion

Satan wants man to believe in evolution and it is Satan's strongest weapon in convincing people that there is no God. Jesus claims to be the truth and the only way to God the Father. <u>John 14:6</u> *"Jesus answered, "I am the way and the truth and the life. No one comes to the Father except through me."* Either Jesus is the greatest liar of all times or He is who He claims to be. What you believe determines if you are a child of God or of Satan!

CHAPTER 4

THE TRUTH WILL SET YOU FREE

Myth # 2: Man has "Freewill" to Choose Christ

Four Major Categories in Man's Decision Making

Does man, according to God's Word, have freewill to choose God/Jesus? Webster's dictionary defines freewill as: ***"Voluntary choice or decision".*** We make decisions momently, many with without much though. I believe that there are four major categories of decision making that man goes through on a daily basis.

1. Physical- Decisions relating to their health i.e. diet; exercise, whether or not to consume alcohol/tobacco and even the amount of sleep one gets. These decisions affect the health of an individual but also require sacrifices if one is to live a healthy life.

2. Financial- Decisions affecting ones long term life style also requires sacrifice by putting off short term gratification for long term gain i.e. higher education, being willing to move

in order to gain a higher/better paying job and even the size of your family.

3. <u>Social</u>- Decisions relating to the people you interact and socialize with, i.e. business associates, friends, family and those you choose not to interact with.

4. <u>Spiritual</u> – Decisions relating to morality, adherence to "Gods Law", and belief in God/Jesus, the creator and sustainer of the universe.

There is no question that man has freewill on all decisions relating to their physical health, financial decisions and social interactions. However, decisions relating to man's spirituality are totally in God's hands. The main question shouldn't be "weather man has the ability to make a decision to believe in God/Jesus", but why God chooses, appoints, calls, elects, or predestines anyone for eternal life in Heaven with Him.

Freewill vs. Predestination

I have struggled with where "freewill" and God's choosing, appointing, calling, election, or predestination intersects. Man not having freewill to make a decision for God/Christ is counterintuitive. Natural man by nature wants to be in control of everything in his/her life. If man actually had the ability to make a decision to accept Christ as their Lord and Savior that would imply that they were more intelligent than those who rejected God/Christ. Pride is something God will not tolerate:

1. <u>Proverbs 16:5</u> *"The Lord detests all the proud of heart. Be sure of this: They will not go unpunished."*

2. <u>Proverbs 8:13</u> *"To fear the LORD is to hate evil; I hate pride and arrogance, evil behavior and perverse speech."*

3. <u>Proverbs 16:18</u> *"Pride goes before destruction, a haughty spirit before a fall."*

Man believing that he has anything to do with his faith /belief in Jesus is pride.

Martin Luther, the great reformer of the Christian Church, clearly stated that there is no such thing as freewill in regard to your salvation. A quote from Martin Luther's book: "The Bondage of the Will" *"Man is by nature as completely unable to know God as to please God."* Luther goes on to say, *"The whole work of man's salvation, first to last, is God's and all the glory for it must be God's also."* Proverbs 14:12 and Proverbs 16:25 *"There is a way that appears to be right to a man, but in the end it leads to death."* The man without God's Spirit will be lost forever by following the world's seductive pleasures!

Sovereign God Determines Mans Fate

The overwhelming evidence is that without man being drawn or enabled, through God's Holy Spirit, no one will ever seek God. Without God's Spirit no one would ever choose God. It is only God's children who receive His gift of His Holy Spirit. We all sin and in God's eyes all sins are equally egregious. God chooses those He imparts faith/belief in Jesus through His Holy Spirit and declares them righteous. Jesus exchanged His righteousness for our sinfulness when He died on the cross.

Satan's children are unable to understand the Bible because they lack God's Holy Spirit. They refuse to accept Jesus' scarifies for the forgiveness of their sins, therefore they must personally pay the price for their sins and endure God's wrath forever.

The Sovereignty of God in the Four Gospels

Following are Jesus' words written by men who lived with Jesus. They witnessed His power, His humility, His death and resurrection from the dead. Most were martyred because they refused to deny Jesus' divinity and resurrection

1. <u>Matthew 22:14</u> *"For many are invited, but few are chosen."* God desires all to come to repentance but He knows of man's evil heart and that only a few will enter through the narrow gate which leads to eternal life.

2. <u>Matthew 15:13</u> *"He replied, "Every plant that my heavenly Father has not planted will be pulled up by the roots."* Man is either of God or of Satan and will live eternally in either Heaven or Hell!

3. <u>Luke 10:22</u> *"All things have been committed to me by my Father. No one knows who the Son is except the Father, and no one knows who the Father is except the Son and those to whom the Son chooses to reveal him."* Jesus gives eternal life to whomever He chooses to reveal himself to, not to everyone.

4. <u>John 5:21</u> *"For just as the Father raises the dead and gives them life, even so the Son gives life to whom he is pleased to give it"* This does not apply to everyone.

5. <u>John 6:37</u> *"All those the Father gives me will come to me, and whoever comes to me I will never drive away."* Believers are given by God to Jesus

6. <u>John 6:44</u> *"No one can come to me unless the Father who sent me draws him, and I will raise him up at the last day."* John went on to say:

7. <u>John 6:65</u> *"This is why I told you that no one can come to me unless the Father has enabled him."* Without God drawing/enabling you, you don't stand a chance of believing in Him.

8. <u>John 8:36</u> *"So if the Son sets you free, you will be free indeed.* Man is incapable of freeing himself of the sinful world without Jesus' help.

9. <u>John 8:47</u> *"He who belongs to God hears what God says. The reason you do not hear is that you do not belong to*

God." Only God's Children here and understand God's message of salvation.

10. John 17:2 *"For you granted him authority over all people that he might give eternal life to all those you have given him."* Salvation was granted to only those given Jesus.

11. John 17:9 *"I am not praying for the world, but for those you have given me, for they are yours.* Jesus is only praying for those who God has given Him.

12. John 17:6 *"I have revealed you to those whom you gave me out of the world. They were yours; you gave them to me and they have obeyed your word."* Again, only those God had given Jesus.

13. John 17:24 *"Father, I want those you have given me to be with me where I am, and to see my glory"*

Additional New Testament Verses

God knows His children, those who He gives to Jesus who will spend eternity with them in Heaven. It is God who chooses whom He will's to forgive, His children, and whom He condemns, Satan's children.

Most of the following verses were written by Paul who prior to his conversion was persecuting followers of Christ. Jesus met him on the road to Damascus and converted him into the greatest evangelist in the Bible. Paul wrote the majority of books in the New Testament. Other New Testament verses:

1. Romans 1:6 *"And you also are among those Gentiles who are called to belong to Jesus Christ."* If you are not called you do not belong to God.

2. Romans 3:11 *"there is no one who understands, no one who seeks God.* If we can't understand God on our own,

God must intervene or the Gospel will be foolishness to everyone.

3. <u>Romans 8:14</u> *"For those who are led by the Spirit of God are the children of God."* Without God's Spirit we are lost and considered children of Satan or anti-Christs.

4. <u>Romans 8:28-31</u> *"And we know that in all things God works for the good of those who love him, who have been called according to his purpose." For those God foreknew he also predestined to be conformed to the image of his Son, that he might be the firstborn among many brothers and sisters. [30] And those he predestined, he also called; those he called, he also justified; those he justified, he also glorified. 31 What, then, shall we say in response to these things? If God is for us, who can be against us?* God is all omniscient and knows the future. Nothing or no one can thwart God's will!

5. <u>Romans 8:33</u> *"Who will bring any charge against those whom God has chosen? It is God who justifies."*

6. <u>Romans 9:11</u> *"Yet, before the twins were born or had done anything good or bad—in order that God's purpose in election might stand: God choose Jacob not Esau even though Esau was born first. not by works but by him who calls—she was told, "The older will serve the younger" [13] Just as it is written: "Jacob I loved, but Esau I hated."* God does the choosing, not man.

7. <u>Romans 11:29</u> *"for God's gifts and his call are irrevocable."* God does not make mistakes!

8. <u>Romans 9:16</u> *"It does not, therefore, depend on human desire or effort, but on God's mercy."* God has mercy only on those He chooses to have mercy!

9. <u>Romans 10:20</u> *"I was found by those who did not seek me; I revealed myself to those who did not ask for me."*

God's gift of His Holy Spirit is the gift of rebirth not given to everyone._

10. Acts 2:39 *"The promise is for you and your children and for all who are far off—for all whom the Lord our God will call."* God's promise was only given to those He chose to call, not everyone.

11. Acts 2:27 *"And the Lord added to their number daily those who were being saved."* It was God, not man adding do their numbers daily.

12. Acts 13:48 *"When the Gentiles heard this, they were glad and honored the word of the Lord; and all who were appointed for eternal life believed."* Only those who were appointed for salvation believed.

13. Acts 26:17-18 *"I will rescue you from your own people and from the Gentiles. I am sending you to them* [18] *to open their eyes and turn them from darkness to light, and from the power of Satan to God, so that they may receive forgiveness of sins and a place among those who are sanctified by faith in me."* Only those who were sanctified by faith in Jesus were rescued.

14. 1st Corinthians 2:5 *"so that your faith might not rest on men's wisdom, but on God's power."* It is all God.

15. 1st Corinthians 3:7 *"So neither he who plants nor he who waters is anything, but only God, who makes things grow."* Only God has the power to grow one's faith into salvation.

16. 1st Corinthians 12:11 *"All these are the work of one and the same Spirit, and he gives them to each one, just as he determines."* God's spirit is given just as God determines, not as man desires.

17. 1 Corinthians 1:23-24 *"but we preach Christ crucified: a stumbling block to Jews and foolishness to Gentiles,* [24] *but*

to those whom God has called, both Jews and Greeks, *Christ the power of God and the wisdom of God.*" It is God's call as to who understands the necessity of Christ's crucifixion for the forgiveness of their sins.

18. 2 Corinthians 1:21-22 *"Now it is God who makes both us and you stand firm in Christ. He anointed us,* [22] *set his seal of ownership on us, and put his Spirit in our hearts as a deposit, guaranteeing what is to come.* It is all God!

19. 2 Corinthians 4:3-4 *"And even if our gospel is veiled, it is veiled to those who are perishing.* [4] *The god of this age has blinded the minds of unbelievers, so that they cannot see the light of the gospel that displays the glory of Christ, who is the image of God".* God blinds those He knows are not His children.

20. Ephesians 4:4 *"There is one body and one Spirit—just as you were called to one hope when you were called."* Only a few are called.

21. 2 Timothy 2:19 *"The Lord knows those who are his,"* and, *"Everyone who confesses the name of the Lord must turn away from wickedness."* God knows His children from Satan's and His children must turn away from sin.

22. Revelation17:14 *"They will wage war against the Lamb, but the Lamb will triumph over them because he is Lord of lords and King of kings—and with him will be his called, chosen and faithful followers."*

23. Revelation 20:15 *"If anyone's name was not found written in the book of life, he was thrown into the lake of fire."* The "book of life" was written before the beginning of time, illustrating that God knew who were to be saved and those who would be lost.

The Sovereignty of God in the Old Testament

Throughout creation, God selected, chose, elected, appointed, called, redeemed or predestined some people to live with Him eternally in Heaven. God is "Holy" which means "separate". He also makes "Holy" or separates His children; His gift of salvation is by grace through faith.

Many Christians have been led to believe that God gave man "freewill" in order that they may, on their own, choose Jesus as their Lord and Savior. Even many Christians today believe that God certainly did not create mankind to be robots. However everything on earth is under God's control:

1. Exodus 4:11 *"The Lord said to him, "Who gave human beings their mouths? Who makes them deaf or mute? Who gives them sight or makes them blind? Is it not I, the Lord?*

2. Deuteronomy 32:39 *"See now that I myself am He! There is no god besides me. I put to death and I bring to life, I have wounded and I will heal, and no one can deliver out of my hand."* Only the creator has the right t to destroy what He has created.

3. 1 Samuel 2:6-7 *"The LORD brings death and makes alive; he brings down to the grave and raises up. [7] The LORD sends poverty and wealth; he humbles and he exalts."*

4. Job 12:23 *"He makes nations great, and destroys them; he enlarges nations, and disperses them."*

5. Psalm 96:13 *"they will sing before the LORD, for he comes, he comes to judge the earth. He will judge the world in righteousness and the peoples in his truth."*

6. Psalm 97:10 *"Let those who love the LORD hate evil, for he guards the lives of his faithful ones and delivers them from the hand of the wicked."*

7. <u>Psalm 115:3</u> *"Our God is in heaven; he does whatever pleases him."*

8. <u>Psalm 135:6</u> *"The LORD does whatever pleases him, in the heavens and on the earth, in the seas and all their depths."*

9. <u>Proverbs 16:4</u> *"The LORD works out everything for his own ends— even the wicked for a day of disaster."* Eventually God will come and judge the world and separate the righteous (His chosen who were given His Holy Spirit) from the wicked.

10. <u>Proverbs 16:9</u> *"In their hearts humans plan their course, but the Lord establishes their steps."* It's all God.

11. <u>Proverbs 16:33</u> *"The lot is cast into the lap, but its every decision is from the LORD."*

12. <u>Proverbs 19:21</u> *"Many are the plans in a man's heart, but it is the LORD's purpose that prevails."*

13. <u>Proverbs 20:24</u> *"A man's steps are directed by the LORD. How then can anyone understand his own way?*

14. <u>Proverbs 21:1</u> *"The king's heart is in the hand of the LORD; he directs it like a watercourse wherever he pleases."*

15. <u>Proverbs 22:2</u> *"Rich and poor have this in common: The LORD is the Maker of them all."*

16. <u>Ecclesiastes 7:14</u> *"When times are good, be happy: but when times are bad, consider: God has made the one as well as the other."* It is all God and man has no say in the matter!

17. <u>Isaiah 45:7</u> *"I form the light and create darkness, I bring prosperity and create disaster; I, the LORD, do all these things."*

18. <u>Isaiah 46:10</u> *"I make known the end from the beginning,*

from ancient times, what is still to come. I say, 'My purpose will stand, and I will do all that I please.

19. <u>Jeremiah 10:23</u> *"I know, O LORD, that a man's life is not his own; it is not for man to direct his steps."*

20. <u>Jeremiah 18:6</u> *"O house of Israel, can I not do with you as this potter does?" declares the LORD. "Like clay in the hand of the potter, so are you in my hand, O house of Israel." disaster comes to a city, has not the LORD caused it?"*

21. <u>Lamentations 3:38</u> *"Is it not from the mouth of the Most High that both calamities and good things come?"*

22. <u>Daniel 2:21</u> *"He changes times and seasons; he deposes kings and raises up others."*

23. <u>Daniel 4:17</u> *"'The decision is announced by messengers, the holy ones declare the verdict, so that the living may know that the Most High is sovereign over all kingdoms on earth and gives them to anyone he wishes and sets over them the lowliest of people."* Sovereign God is in control of everything!

24. <u>Daniel 4:35</u> *"All the peoples of the earth are regarded as nothing. He does as he pleases with the powers of heaven and the peoples of the earth. No one can hold back his hand or say to him: "What have you done?*

God's Choices in the Past

Although you are able to choose your spouse and friends, God chose your parents and where you were born! It makes a major difference as to who your parents were/are and where you were born. Do you think someone born in a Moslem country to radical extremist parents would have the same chance of becoming a Christian as someone born to Christian parents in the USA? However, this is possible if our sovereign

God wills it to happen! That is why God send out missionaries in order to reach God's children throughout the world.

It is God who decides who He will have compassion on and who He will harden or condemn. God's sovereignty and control over everything allows Him to both love some unconditionally, His children, while creating a place where Satan and his followers will be separated from Him eternally in Hell.

Verses regarding God's choosing/sovereignty in the Old Testament:

1. Genesis 18:19 *"For I have chosen him, so that he will direct his children and his household after him to keep the way of the LORD by doing what is right and just, so that the LORD will bring about for Abraham what he has promised him."* God chose the Jews over all other people of the world.

2. Exodus 15:13 *"In your unfailing love you will lead the people you have redeemed. In your strength you will guide them to your holy dwelling.* It only mentions those God has redeemed.

3. Deuteronomy 7:6 *"For you are a people holy to the LORD your God. The LORD your God has chosen you out of all the peoples on the face of the earth to be his people, his treasured possession."*

4. Psalm 33:12 *"Blessed is the nation whose God is the LORD, the people he chose for his inheritance."*

5. Psalm 4:3 *"Know that the Lord has set apart his faithful servant for himself; the Lord hears when I call to him".* God's word is very clear regarding His choosing, election, calling, redeeming or predestinating of His children. They will live with Him in Heaven forever.

6. Psalm 105:26 *"He sent Moses his servant, and Aaron, whom he had chosen."*

7. Psalm 78:67-68 *"Then he rejected the tents of Joseph, he*

did not choose the tribe of Ephraim; [68] *but he chose the tribe of Judah, Mount Zion, which he loved."*

8. Psalm 78:70 *"He chose David his servant and took him from the sheep pens;"*

9. Psalms 65:4 *"Blessed are those you choose and bring near to live in your courts!"* Not because they were better, stronger or more faithful than any other nation but because God is sovereign.

10. Psalm 37:22 *"those the Lord blesses will inherit the land, but those he curses will be destroyed."* Not everyone is blessed but those whom God chooses.

11. Psalm 65:4 *"Blessed are those you choose and bring near to live in your courts!"*

12. Amos 3:2 *"You only have I chosen of all the families of the earth;* God is talking about the nation Israel.

13. Isaiah 41:8-9 *"But you, O Israel, my servant, Jacob, whom I have chosen, you descendants of Abraham my friend,* [9] *I took you from the ends of the earth, from its farthest corners I called you. I said, 'You are my servant'; I have chosen you and have not rejected you."*

God changed Jacob's name to Israel. He foretold of the conflict between Jacob with His brother Esau back in: Genesis 25:23 *"The Lord said to her, "Two nations are in your womb, and two peoples from within you will be separated; one people will be stronger than the other, and the older will serve the younger."* As God predicted, all this happened many years later. God changed Jacobi's name to Israel the name of the Jewish nation 3000 years ago and remains Israel today.

Believers were Chosen Before the Creation of the World

Throughout the Bible God states that His elect, chosen, called, appointed, redeemed or those He predestined were selected by His divine sovereignty and they were chosen before the world came into existence!

1. Psalm 139:16 *"Your eyes saw my unformed body; all the days ordained for me were written in your book before one of them came to be."*

2. Proverbs 8:23 *"I was formed long ages ago, at the very beginning, when the world came to be."*

3. Psalm 139:4 *"Before a word is on my tongue you, Lord, know it completely Lord".*

4. Ephesians 1:4-5 *"For he chose us in him before the creation of the world to be holy and blameless in his sight. In love ⁵he predestined us to be adopted as his sons through Jesus Christ, in accordance with his pleasure and will"* _

5. Matthew 25:34 *"Then the King will say to those on his right, 'Come, you who are blessed by my Father; take your inheritance, the kingdom prepared for you since the creation of the world."* _

6. 2 Timothy 1:9 *This grace was given us in Christ Jesus before the beginning of time".*

7. Revelations 17:8 *"The inhabitants of the earth whose names have not been written in the book of life from the creation of the world will be astonished when they see the beast, because it once was, now is not, and yet will come."* If your name is not in "The Book of Life" you are not God's child. Therefore, if God chose us before the creation of the world, how can I make a decision to choose Him? Is man able to thwart God's will?

Sovereign God Does the Choosing, Not Man

It is God who through choosing, election, calling, appointing or because of His "foreknowledge" that man is saved.

1. John 3:27 *"To this John replied, "A person can receive only what is given them from heaven."*

2. Hebrews 9:15 *"For this reason Christ is the mediator of a new covenant, that those who are called may receive the promised eternal inheritance—now that he has died as a ransom to set them free from the sins committed under the first covenant."* It is only those who are called that receive God's forgiveness.

3. Ephesians 1:11 *"In him we were also chosen, having been predestined according to the plan of him who works out everything in conformity with the purpose of his will,"* It is God's will not our intellect as to why we are chosen..

4. Ecclesiastes 9:1 *"So I reflected on all this and concluded that the righteous and the wise and what they do are in God's hands, but no man knows whether love or hate awaits him."*

5. Hebrews 9:28 *"so Christ was sacrificed once to take away the sins of many; and he will appear a second time, not to bear sin, but to bring salvation to those who are waiting for him."* Unbelievers are not waiting for Jesus' return.

6. Peter 1:1-2 *"Peter, an apostle of Jesus Christ, To God's elect, exiles scattered throughout the provinces of Pontus, Galatia, Cappadocia, Asia and Bithynia, ² who have been chosen according to the foreknowledge of God the Father, through the sanctifying work of the Spirit, to be obedient to Jesus Christ and sprinkled with his blood: Grace and peace be yours in abundance."* It is God's elect, according to His foreknowledge, not man's choosing.

7. <u>Galatians 1:11</u> *"Paul, an apostle—sent not from men nor by a man, but by Jesus Christ and God the Father"* Paul was chosen by God, Paul didn't choose Him.

8. <u>Galatians 1:15</u> *"But when God, who set me apart from my mother's womb and called me by his grace"* Paul was set apart for God before he was born.

9. <u>1 John 3:24</u> *"The one who keeps God's commands lives in him, and he in them. And this is how we know that he lives in us: We know it by the Spirit he gave us."* God's Spirit is a gift from God, not given to everyone.

Salvation Requires Rebirth

Without God's Spirit no one will come to faith in Jesus. God's Holy Spirit is the means by which God makes Himself known to His chosen people. Without God's Holy Spirit the Bible is foolishness. Only through the miracle of God's grace and mercy can our dead spirit come to life. An acronym for Grace" is:

<u>G</u>od's <u>R</u>iches <u>A</u>t <u>C</u>hrist's <u>E</u>xpense.

Claiming to know God will not save you for even Satan's demons know that God exists. <u>James 2:19</u> *"You believe that there is one God. Good! Even the demons believe that—and shudder"* The only way for someone to enter the Kingdom of God is to be born again, born of the Spirit.

Man has freewill to sin which we all do often. Unless God gives life to your dead spirit you will be God's enemy, we are all dead to sin from birth:

1. <u>John 3:3</u> *"In reply Jesus declared, "I tell you the truth, no one can see the kingdom of God unless he is born again."* Rebirth is God opening one's eyes to understanding His Word through His Holy Spirit.

2. <u>John 3:5-6</u> *"Jesus answered, "Very truly I tell you, no*

one can enter the kingdom of God unless they are born of water and the Spirit. [6] *Flesh gives birth to flesh, but the Spirit gives birth to spirit."* However, in God's mercy and grace, He chooses to saves some from eternal separation from Him

3. Romans 8:9 *"And if anyone does not have the Spirit of Christ, they do not belong to Christ."* No one without God's Holy Spirit is a child of God.

4. Ephesian 2:1 *"As for you, you were dead in your transgressions and sins,"* Only God can raise one's dead spirit. A dead man can't bring his dead spirit to life!

5. 1 Corinthians 1:18 *"For the message of the cross is foolishness to those who are perishing, but to us who are being saved it is the power of God."* God's elect, appointed, chosen, called or predestined are His children and given His gift of His Holy Spirit.

6. 1 Corinthians 1:24 *"but to those whom God has called, both Jews and Greeks, Christ the power of God and the wisdom of God."* However, you must be called.

7. 2 Thessalonians 2:10-12 *"and all the ways that wickedness deceives those who are perishing. They perish because they refused to love the truth and so be saved.* [11] *For this reason God sends them a powerful delusion so that they will believe the lie* [12] *and so that all will be condemned who have not believed the truth but have delighted in wickedness."* God will send a "powerful delusion" to the wicked that are perishing, the lost.

8. 2nd Corinthians 5:17-18 *"Therefore, if anyone is in Christ, he is a new creation; the old has gone, the new has come!* [18]*All this is from God, who reconciled us to himself through Christ and gave us the ministry of reconciliation"* If there is no change in one's life there is no rebirth.

9. <u>1 John 5:1</u> *"Everyone who believes that Jesus is the Christ is born of God and everyone who loves the father loves his child as well."*

Only the Holy Spirit can enables a man to believe that Jesus suffered, died and paid the full price for all man's sins. This concept makes no sense to Satan's followers, those who are perishing.

It is all by God's Grace

Every one sins and it is only through God's mercy and grace that anyone is saved. It is not up to man to judge God's choices or motives. Instead of focusing on why God does not chose to save some, consider why God chose to save anyone.

1. <u>Isaiah 64:6</u> *"All of us have become like one who is unclean, and all our righteous acts are like filthy rags; we all shrivel up like a leaf, and like the wind our sins sweep us away"* However, due to God's mercy and grace God chooses to save His children, believers.

2. <u>Ephesians 2:1-5</u> *"As for you, you were dead in your transgressions and sins, ²in which you used to live when you followed the ways of this world and of the ruler of the kingdom of the air, the spirit who is now at work in those who are disobedient. ³All of us also lived among them at one time, gratifying the cravings of our sinful nature] and following its desires and thoughts. Like the rest, we were by nature objects of wrath. ⁴But because of his great love for us, God, who is rich in mercy, ⁵made us alive with Christ even when we were dead in transgressions—it is by grace you have been saved."*

3. <u>Colossians 2:13</u> *"When you were dead in your sins and in the uncircumcision of your sinful nature, God made you alive with Christ. He forgave us all our sins,"* God made

His children alive through the gift of His Spirit; dead people are unable to come to life without God's miracle of rebirth.

4. Ephesians 2:8-9 *"For it is by grace you have been saved, through faith—and this is not from yourselves, it is the gift of God—* [9] *not by works, so that no one can boast."*

5. 1st Corinthians 15:10 *"But by the grace of God I am what I am, and his grace to me was not without effect. No, I worked harder than all of them—yet not I, but the grace of God that was with me."* Paul states that only by God's grace is Paul who he is._

6. 2nd Timothy 1:9 *"who has saved us and called us to a holy life—not because of anything we have done but because of his own purpose and grace. This grace was given us in Christ Jesus before the beginning of time,"*

7. Romans 11:5 *"So too, at the present time there is a remnant chosen by grace."* The remnant Paul is talking about iare God's chosen or elect! It is a gift given by God to His children only._

Man's Need for the Holy Spirit

Being born again not only results in accepting Jesus as Lord and Savior, but also, in a changed life. Born again Christians are to flee from sin and repent from their past sinful behavior. If your life doesn't radically change after accepting Christ as your Lord and Savior, then you are deceiving yourself into a false sense of salvation. So called Christians that live lives that can't be distinguished from unbelievers lives are going to be disappointed when Jesus says, *"depart from me, I don't know you"*.

Following are many Bible verses illustrating the need for the Holy Spirit in order to understand God's will and to be saved:

1. Romans 8:5-10 *"Those who live according to the sinful nature have their minds set on what that nature desires; but those who live in accordance with the Spirit have their minds set on what the Spirit desires. [6]The mind of sinful man is death, but the mind controlled by the Spirit is life and peace; [7]the sinful mind is hostile to God. It does not submit to God's law, nor can it do so. [8]Those controlled by the sinful nature cannot please God.9 You, however, are controlled not by the sinful nature but by the Spirit, if the Spirit of God lives in you. And if anyone does not have the Spirit of Christ, he does not belong to Christ. [10]But if Christ is in you, your body is dead because of sin, yet your spirit is alive because of righteousness."* Death is only temporary. All people will eventually live eternally in either Heaven or Hell.

2. Romans 8:13-14 *"For if you live according to the sinful nature, you will die; but if by the Spirit you put to death the misdeeds of the body, you will live, [14]because those who are led by the Spirit of God are sons of God."*

3. Romans 11:5-8 *"So too, at the present time there is a remnant chosen by grace. [6]And if by grace, then it cannot be based on works; if it were, grace would no longer be grace.[7] What then? What the people of Israel sought so earnestly they did not obtain. The elect among them did, but the others were hardened, [8] as it is written: "God gave them a spirit of stupor, eyes that could not see and ears that could not hear, to this very day."* Salvation is all by God's grace.

Jesus Chose His Disciples and some for Healing

Jesus chose his disciples and He also chose many other sinners in order to reveal Himself as the "Christ" and savior of the world. Mark 2:14

"As he walked along, he saw Levi son of Alphaeus sitting at the tax collector's booth. "Follow me," Jesus told him, and Levi got up and followed him. Levi was a hated tax collector and would be one of the last persons that anyone would expect to be a child of God. Levi did nothing to earn Jesus' attention but Jesus asked him to follow Him and he became one of His loyal disciples.

Jesus chose to heal many severely handicapped people, both physically and spiritually. John 5:5-6 *"One who was there had been an invalid for thirty-eight years. ⁶When Jesus saw him lying there and learned that he had been in this condition for a long time, he asked him, "Do you want to get well?"* John 9:1-3 *"As he went along, he saw a man blind from birth. ²His disciples asked him, "Rabbi, who sinned, this man or his parents, that he was born blind?" ³"Neither this man nor his parents sinned," said Jesus, "but this happened so that the work of God might be displayed in his life."* Jesus chose to heal these men so as to reveal himself as God's Messiah, His anointed one.

Moses' Attempt to Resist God

Moses tried to resist God's calling to bring the people out of Egypt. Exodus 3:10 *"So now, go. I am sending you to Pharaoh to bring my people the Israelites out of Egypt."* Moses did everything possible to talk God out of using him to free the Israelites. Exodus 3:11 *"But Moses said to God, "Who am I that I should go to Pharaoh and bring the Israelites out of Egypt?"* God's answer was that He would be with Him and He wouldn't take no for an answer:

1. Exodus 3:13 *"Moses said to God, "Suppose I go to the Israelites and say to them, 'The God of your fathers has sent me to you,' and they ask me, 'What is his name?' Then what shall I tell them?"* God's answer was "I AM" has sent me to you." "I AM" is how God defined Himself to His people.

2. <u>Exodus 4:1</u> *"Moses answered, "What if they do not believe me or listen to me and say, 'The LORD did not appear to you'?"* Then God preformed a miracle and changed Moses staff into a snake.

3. <u>Exodus 4:10-11</u> *"Moses said to the LORD, "Pardon your servant, Lord. I have never been eloquent, neither in the past nor since you have spoken to your servant. I am slow of speech and tongue."*[11] *The LORD said to him, "Who gave human beings their mouths? Who makes them deaf or mute? Who gives them sight or makes them blind? Is it not I, the LORD?*

4. <u>Exodus 4:13</u> *"But Moses said, "Pardon your servant, Lord. Please send someone else."* You know the rest of the story; Moses finally obeyed God and accomplished His will.

Jonah's Attempt to Escape from God

Jonah also tried to resist God's instructions when God commanded Jonah to go and preach to Israel's hated enemy, the people of Nineveh. <u>Jonah 1:2-3</u> *"Go to the great city of Nineveh and preach against it, because its wickedness has come up before me."* [3] *But Jonah ran away from the LORD and headed for Tarshish. He went down to Joppa, where he found a ship bound for that port. After paying the fare, he went aboard and sailed for Tarshish to flee from the LORD.* Instead of following God's order, Jonah went in the opposite direction.

God caused a great storm and Jonah was thrown overboard. He was swallowed by a great fish and after 3 days he was taken to where the Lord commanded him to go in the first place. <u>Jonah 3:1-3</u> *"Then the word of the LORD came to Jonah a second time:* [2] *"Go to the great city of Nineveh and proclaim to it the message I give you."* [3] *Jonah obeyed the word of the LORD and went to Nineveh."* The point is that no man can resist God's will.

Saul's Persecution of Christians and Conversion

Saul, later called Paul, was an enemy of the church and was persecuting new Christian believers. He even participated in the stoning of Steven. God got his attention by knocking him to the ground and blinding him.

1. Acts 9:5-6 *"Who are you, Lord?" Saul asked. "I am Jesus, whom you are persecuting," he replied.* [6] *"Now get up and go into the city, and you will be told what you must do."* God had plans for Saul.

2. Acts 9:15-16 *"But the Lord said to Ananias, "Go! This man is my chosen instrument to proclaim my name to the Gentiles and their kings and to the people of Israel.* [16] *I will show him how much he must suffer for my name."* Do you think that Paul could have refused god's calling? No one suffered more for the faith than Paul. 2 Corinthians 11:23-28 *"I have worked much harder, been in prison more frequently, been flogged more severely, and been exposed to death again and again.* [24] *Five times I received from the Jews the forty lashes minus one.* [25] *Three times I was beaten with rods, once I was pelted with stones, three times I was shipwrecked, I spent a night and a day in the open sea,* [26] *I have been constantly on the move. I have been in danger from rivers, in danger from bandits, in danger from my fellow Jews, in danger from Gentiles; in danger in the city, in danger in the country, in danger at sea; and in danger from false believers.* [27] *I have labored and toiled and have often gone without sleep; I have known hunger and thirst and have often gone without food; I have been cold and naked.* [28] *Besides everything else, I face daily the pressure of my concern for all the churches."* In spite of all this, Paul was faithful because God was encouraging him along the way. In order

to encourage Paul, God showed him the Third Heaven which was beyond Paul's wildest imagination.

3. <u>2 Corinthians 12:2-4</u> *"I know a man in Christ who fourteen years ago was caught up to the third heaven. Whether it was in the body or out of the body I do not know—God knows.* [3] *And I know that this man— whether in the body or apart from the body I do not know, but God knows—* [4] *was caught up to paradise and heard inexpressible things, things that no one is permitted to tell."*

God chose Abraham, Joseph, Moses, David and many others even though they were sinners. Does anyone believe that any of the above people could refuse God's calling?

Moses was a murderer and David was an adulterer and a murderer. God chose the weaker, the flawed people in order to demonstrate His power over man's weakness. This offers hope for sinners like me and you. <u>Deuteronomy 9:6</u> *"Understand, then, that it is not because of your righteousness that the LORD your God is giving you this good land to possess, for you are a stiff-necked people."* Often we get what we don't deserve.

Satan's Attempt to Turn Job Away from God

Job is an example of Satan believing that he could turn Job away from God by removing all God's blessings on him. God gave Satan permission to do what he wanted to do to Job except touching him physically. <u>Job 1:12:</u> *The LORD said to Satan, "very well, then, everything he has in your power, but on the man himself do not lay a finger." Then Satan went out from the presence of the LORD."* Job lost everything he had including all his children. Jobs response: <u>Job 1:20-21</u> *"At this, Job got up and tore his robe and shaved his head. Then he fell to the ground in worship* [21] *and said: "Naked I came from my mother's womb, and naked I will depart. The LORD gave and the LORD has taken away; may the name of the LORD be praised."*

Next Satan got permission from God to inflict Job with "painful sores from the soles of his feet to the top of his head." In spite of all this, Job still did not disparage God even though his wife said: Job 2:9-10 *"His wife said to him, "Are you still maintaining your integrity? Curse God and die!"* [10] *He replied, "You are talking like a foolish woman. Shall we accept good from God, and not trouble?" In all this, Job did not sin in what he said."*

After all that happened to Job, he never gave in to Satan. Job 42:1-2 *"Then Job replied to the LORD:* [2] *"I know that you can do all things; no purpose of yours can be thwarted."* I could go on and on with many additional people like Joseph, Gideon, all the prophets etc. The main point is to expose through scripture that no purpose of the God can or will be thwarted. This was true for Moses, Jonah, Paul, Job and many others.

All Have Sinned!

Since we all sin and in God's eyes all sins, white lies and murder, are equally egregious. How can anyone be saved other than through God's mercy and grace?

1. Ecclesiastes 7:20 *"There is not a righteous man on earth who does what is right and never sins."*

2. Psalm 51:5 *"Surely I was sinful at birth, sinful from the time my mother conceived me."*

3. Psalm 58:3 *"Even from birth the wicked go astray; from the womb they are wayward, spreading lies.*

4. Psalm 14:13 *"The fool says in his heart, "There is no God." They are corrupt, their deeds are vile; there is no one who does good.*[2] *The LORD looks down from heaven on the sons of men to see if there are any who*

understand, any who seek God. [3] *All have turned aside, they have together become corrupt; there is no one who does good, not even one."*

5.   <u>Romans 3:10-12</u> *"As it is written: "There is no one righteous, not even one;* [11] *there is no one who understands; there is no one who seeks God.* [12] *All have turned away, they have together become worthless; there is no one who does good, not even one."*

6.   <u>Psalm 143:2</u> *"Do not bring your servant into judgment, for no one living is righteous before you"* It is beyond comprehension why the powerful creator of everything would sacrifice His only Son for selfish/sinful man. However God choses to save some by giving them His Holy Spirit so they will accept Jesus's sacrifice on the cross, exchanging our sinfulness for Jesus' righteous.

Who Would Choose Hell over Heaven?

What are 100 years of a comfortable, enjoyable life here on earth vs. billions and billions of years in hell? Everyone would choose heaven, where there is total eternal bliss, and a peace that passes all understanding with no sickness, suffering or decay. Contrast that with Hell where you suffer God's eternal wrath. You burn with a fire that never goes out, you wish you would die but you suffer forever.

It doesn't take a rocket scientist to choose heaven if one truly believed there was a Hell for Satan and his followers. The greedy, the self-centered, the intellects of this world would do whatever was necessary in order to earn eternity in Heaven. However, because of their disbelief they are the condemned and will spend eternity in Hell.

Who's Child are You?

Every person not chosen, called, elected, appointed or predestined by God, are considered to be a children of Satan and will be uprooted and thrown into the lake of fire._

1. John 1:12-13 *"Yet to all who did receive him, to those who believed in his name, he gave the right to become children of God— [13] children born not of natural descent, nor of human decision or a husband's will, but born of God."* Note they are not of human decision but born of God. Without God's Spirit man will never know God and will be separated from Him eternally._

2. Matthew 13:37-42 *"He answered, "The one who sowed the good seed is the Son of Man. [38] The field is the world, and the good seed stands for the people of the kingdom. The weeds are the people of the evil one, [39] and the enemy who sows them is the devil. The harvest is the end of the age, and the harvesters are angels. [40] "As the weeds are pulled up and burned in the fire, so it will be at the end of the age. [41] The Son of Man will send out his angels, and they will weed out of his kingdom everything that causes sin and all who do evil. [42] They will throw them into the blazing furnace, where there will be weeping and gnashing of teeth.* Jesus explained this parable of the wheat and weeds by stating that the wheat represented "good seed" or the "sons of the kingdom" or the children of God. The weeds represented the "sons of the evil one" or children of Satan.

3. Matthew 25:41 *"Then he will say to those on his left, 'Depart from me, you who are cursed, into the eternal fire prepared for the devil and his angels."* Many people will be disappointed when they are thrown into Hell because of their lacked of faith/belief._

4. John 8:47 *"Whoever belongs to God hears what God says. The reason you do not hear is that you do not belong to God."*

5. John 8:43 *"Why is my language not clear to you? Because you are unable to hear what I say.*

6. John 10:3-5 *"The gatekeeper opens the gate for him, and the sheep listen to his voice. He calls his own sheep by name and leads them out. ⁴ When he has brought out all his own, he goes on ahead of them, and his sheep follow him because they know his voice. ⁵ But they will never follow a stranger; in fact, they will run away from him because they do not recognize a stranger's voice."*

7. John 10:14 *"I am the good shepherd; I know my sheep and my sheep know me"* However, children of Satan do not believe in Jesus because they are not one of His sheep.

8. John 10:26-28 *"but you do not believe because you are not my sheep. ²⁷ My sheep listen to my voice; I know them, and they follow me. ²⁸ I give them eternal life, and they shall never perish; no one will snatch them out of my hand."* The lost or children of Satan don't hear or understand God's Word therefore they will spend eternity in Hell separated from God..

9. Romans 8:16 *"The Spirit himself testifies with our spirit that we are God's children."* Jesus calls His children His Sheep. They know His voice and follow only Him.

10. Romans 9:11-13 *"Yet, before the twins were born or had done anything good or bad—in order that God's purpose in election might stand: ¹²not by works but by him who calls—she was told, "The older will serve the younger," ¹³Just as it is written: "Jacob I loved, but Esau I hated."*

11. Hebrews 9:15 *"For this reason Christ is the mediator of a new covenant, that those who are called may receive the*

promised eternal inheritance—now that he has died as a ransom to set them free from the sins committed under the first covenant." "Those who are called" is repeated over and over throughout scripture. If you are not called you can't and will not respond to God's message of redemption.

God's children, the saved, are aware of their sinful nature and repent when they become aware of their sins by turning away from their sin and back to God. Although true Christians continue to sin, they know they are forgiven through the shed blood of their Lord and Savior Jesus.

Martin Luther's Convictions

Martin Luther was a famous German theologian, Biblical scholar, author and leader in the Protestant Reformation. His book, "The Bondage of the Will" is still required reading for most Lutheran seminary students today. Luther proved through his understanding of scripture that there was no such thing as "free will". Luther states in his book:

1. *"Man is by nature as completely unable to know God as to please God; let him face the fact and admit it! Let God be God and man be man."*

2. *"The whole work of man's salvation, first to last, is God's and all the glory for it must be God's also."*

3. *"But it is only through Christ that God wills to be known, and gives saving knowledge of Himself. He who would know God, therefore, must seek Him through the Biblical gospel. We must not expect to understand all that the gospel tells us, for the fact of Christ (that is, the achievement of our salvation by the death of incarnate Son of God) is beyond man's rational comprehension."*

4. *"The Creator directly energizes and controls all the*

acts of His creatures. All events are necessitated by His immutable, sovereign will."

5. *"For to rely on oneself for faith is no different in principle from relying on oneself for works, and the one is as un-Christian and anti-Christian as the other."*

6. *"The truth is that nobody who has not the Spirit of God sees a jot of what is in the Scriptures. All men have their hearts darkened, so that, even when they can discuss and quote all that is in Scripture, they do not understand or really know any of it."*

7. *It is, then, fundamentally necessary and wholesome for Christians to know that God foreknows nothing contingently, but that He foresees, purposes, and does all things according to His own immutable, eternal and infallible will."*

8. *For if you hesitate to believe, or are too proud to acknowledge, that God foreknows and wills all things, not contingently, but necessarily and immutably, how can you believe, trust and rely on His promises?"* Luther goes on to say that we are not entitled to edit and reduce God's Word so as to make it square with our own preconceived ideas.

9. *"That, again, is to try and make man into God, for to understand all thing perfectly, is the prerogative of the Creator alone. And it is also to exclude faith; for the very distinguishing mark of faith is that it takes God's word just because it is God's word, whether or not it can at present understand it. Man's part, therefore, is to humble his proud mind, to renounce the sinful self-sufficiency which prompts him to treat himself as the measure of all things, to confess the blindness of his corrupt heart and thankfully to receive the enlightening Word of God. Man is by nature as completely unable to know God as*

to please God; let him face the fact and admit it! Let God be God!"

Just because we don't understand God's ways we shouldn't question Him and as Luther said, *"let God be God"*!

Other Pastor's Opinions

In John MacArthur's book "Hard to Believe" he states: *"if Christians don't acknowledge and preach the fact that salvation is through Christ alone, they are herding unwittingly people through the wide gate that leads to destruction."* John goes on to say: *"When you come to brokenness, the recognition that you, of yourself, cannot make it through the narrow gate, then Christ pours into you grace upon grace to strengthen you for that entrance, In your brokenness, His power becomes your resource. Our part is to admit our sin and inability and plead for mercy and power from on high."*

In another of John MacArthur's books "The Gospel According to Jesus" he says: *"Let me say as clearly as possible right now that salvation is by God's sovereign grace and grace alone. Nothing a lost, degenerate, spiritually dead sinner can do will in any way contribute to salvation. Saving faith, repentance, commitment, and obedience are all divine works, wrought by the Holy Spirit in the heart of everyone who is saved."* John goes on to say: *"real salvation cannot, and will not, fail to produce works of righteousness in the life of a true believer."*

No one will ever be able to "earn" salvation because we all sin. Jesus paid the price for all sins through His sacrifice on the cross. However, those who deny Jesus are condemned and they will die in there sins and spend eternity in Hell..

77

Love God and Hate the World

We are to love God more than anything or anyone in the world. Conforming to the sinful world which is in Satan control is the road that leads to Hell:

1. James 4:4 *"You adulterous people, don't you know that friendship with the world is hatred toward God?"* Anyone who chooses to be a friend of the world is an enemy of God.

2. John 15:19 *"If you belonged to the world, it would love you as its own. As it is, you do not belong to the world, but I have chosen you out of the world. That is why the world hates you.* Those who stand for truth are hated by the world!

3. Matthew 10:32-34 *"Whoever acknowledges me before others, I will also acknowledge before my Father in heaven. [33] But whoever disowns me before others, I will disown before my Father in heaven".* The world is very seductive and the reason most people follow the world rather than God. Most people would rather receive the praise of man than of God.

4. Matthew 6:24 *"No one can serve two masters. Either you will hate the one and love the other, or you will be devoted to the one and despise the other. You cannot serve both God and money.* We are to love God more than our parents our spouse and our children. Anything we put in front of God is "idol worship"!

5. Luke 14:26 *"If anyone comes to me and does not hate his father and mother, his wife and children, his brothers and sisters—yes, even his own life—he cannot be my disciple."* I believe that hate here is used for emphasis implying the importance of putting God 1st in your life.

God's Elect or Chosen

God's elect will be gathered together someday and spend eternity in heaven as His beloved children. It is a deadly mistake to think that God will save everyone. Here He only speaks of His "elect".

1. <u>Matthew 24:31</u> *"And he will send his angels with a loud trumpet call, and they will gather his elect from the four winds, from one end of the heavens to the other."*

2. <u>Mark 13:20</u> *"If the Lord had not cut short those days, no one would survive. But for the sake of the elect, whom he has chosen, he has shortened them".*

3. <u>Mark 13:27</u> *"And he will send his angels and gather his elect from the four winds, from the ends of the earth to the ends of the heavens."*

4. <u>1 Peter 1:1-2</u> *"Peter, an apostle of Jesus Christ, To God's elect, strangers in the world, scattered throughout Pontus, Galatia, Cappadocia, Asia and Bithynia, [2]who have been chosen according to the foreknowledge of God the Father, through the sanctifying work of the Spirit, for obedience to Jesus Christ and sprinkling by his blood:*

5. *"*<u>Psalm 33:12</u> *"Blessed is the nation whose God is the LORD, the people he chose for his inheritance".*

Paul devoted his life for the sake of God's "elect" or His chosen. <u>2 Timothy 2:10</u> *"Therefore I endure everything for the sake of the elect, that they too may obtain the salvation that is in Christ Jesus, with eternal glory."*

God is "Omniscient"

Not only is God all powerful and sovereign, He is omniscient and knows everything. Some may argue that God's foreknowledge may be the reason He chooses those He knew would accept and believe in Him. Weather it is because God is omniscient or that some people are predestined for salvation, it still is all God!

The Bible makes it clear that we all sin and deserve God's wrath. Our concern should not be why God doesn't save everyone but to be thankful that God saved a wretch like me! God knows the future and everything about us:

1. <u>Matthew 10:29-30</u> *"Are not two sparrows sold for a penny? Yet not one of them will fall to the ground apart from the will of your Father. [30]And even the very hairs of your head are all numbered."*

2. <u>Psalms 139:1-4</u> *"O LORD, you have searched me and you know me. [2] You know when I sit and when I rise; you perceive my thoughts from afar. [3] You discern my going out and my lying down; you are familiar with all my ways. [4]Before a word is on my tongue you know it completely, O LORD"*

God's Thoughts are Beyond our Comprehension

The mind of the "creator of everything" cannot be compared with the mind of man:

1. <u>Romans11:33-36</u> *"Oh, the depth of the riches of the wisdom and knowledge of God! How unsearchable his judgments, and his paths beyond tracing out![34]"Who has known the mind of the Lord? Or who has been his counselor?" [35]"Who has ever given to God, that God should repay him?" [36]For from him and through him and to him are all things. To him be the glory forever! Amen.*

2. *"*<u>Isaiah 55:8-9</u> *"For my thoughts are not your thoughts, neither are your ways my ways," declares the LORD. [9] "As the heavens are higher than the earth, so are my*

ways higher than your ways and my thoughts than your thoughts."!

Seek God and His Righteousness

The most important thing a believer should do is to continually seek God by studying His word, and seek His righteousness by keeping His commandments:

1. Matthew 6:33 *"But seek first his kingdom and his righteousness, and all these things will be given to you as well. ³⁴Therefore do not worry about tomorrow, for tomorrow will worry about itself. Each day has enough trouble of its own."* If we truly love God/Jesus we will obey His commandments. However, we all will fall short of God's desired perfection.

2. John 14:15 *"If you love me, keep my commands."*

3. John 15:10 *"If you keep my commands, you will remain in my love, just as I have kept my Father's commands and remain in his love."* Do we truly love God if we knowingly continually, disobey His commands? _

4. Matthew 12:30 *"He who is not with me is against me, and he who does not gather with me scatters."* There is no "middle ground" in faith or belief. If you are not for Jesus than you are against Him!

Gifts vs. Wages

A gift is something freely given as an expression of love and gratitude. A wage is something that is earned, expected and deserved. How you view your life determines whether you consider your successes as "gifts from God" or "wages" things you have earned through hard work and therefore you deserve them:

1. James 1:17 *"Every good and perfect gift is from above, coming down from the Father of the heavenly lights, who does not change like shifting shadows."*

2. John 3:27 *"To this John replied, "A person can receive only what is given them from heaven."* Christianly is the only religion that does not require works or good deeds in order to earn your salvation.

3. Ephesians 2:8-10 *"For it is by grace you have been saved, through faith—and this is not from yourselves, it is the gift of God—* [9] *not by works, so that no one can boast.* [10] *For we are God's handiwork, created in Christ Jesus to do good works, which God prepared in advance for us to do."*

It was only by God reaching down to sinful man and exchanging our sinfulness for Jesus's righteousness that anyone is saved! Jesus' shed blood covers all believers' sins, past, present and future. Every other religion requires "works" as man has to earn his/her salvation

Three Protestant Views Regarding Freewill

There are three different protestant views relating to how the Holy Spirit works regarding one's salvation, the belief in the saving work of Christ:

1. Decision Theology- That man on his own can and does have the ability to make a conscious decision to accept Jesus as Lord and savior. This view is held by many Baptist, Non-denominational and Pentecostal churches. Churches that believe in "decision theology" usually have "alter calls" where members, after believing the Gospel message verbally proclaim Christ as their Lord and savior.

2. <u>Limited Free Will</u>- This teaching is held by the Lutheran Church which as Martin Luther wrote, "I cannot by my own reason or strength, believe in Jesus Christ my Lord or come to Him". They believe that faith in Christ is only the work of the Holy Spirit and has nothing to do with man's desire or actions. It is limited free will because Lutherans believe people also have free will to later reject the Gospel message.

3. <u>One Work</u>- This teaching has its roots in John Kalvin and is common in Presbyterian, Methodist, and Anglican Churches. They believe that not only is faith/belief in Christ totally the work of the Holy Spirit but that once you are saved, you may never be able to loose faith or apostasy. Not only do they believe that salvation is all the work of the Holy Spirit but also that once you are saved, you could never fall away from God's grace.

What your church believes in has a direct effect on how it shares the Gospel message with its people. However, in all three views, the Gospel must be preached in order to reach sinful man! Weather you believe man has the ability on his/her own to accept the Gospel message or that only through God's election, being chosen, called, appointed or predestined that he/she is able to become children of God. The key ingredient in all three instances is <u>faith/belief</u>! <u>John 3:18</u> ***"Whoever believes in him is not condemned, but whoever does not believe stands condemned already because they have not believed in the name of God's one and only Son."***

Bible Verses that Support "Decision Theology"

There are two key verses that seem to indicate that man can actually choose God. The first verse is a recommendation for the people of Israel to choose life rather than death. Although many churches promote "decision theology", the Bible clearly states belief/faith is totally up to God.

1. Deuteronomy 30:19 *"This day I call the heavens and the earth as witnesses against you that I have set before you life and death, blessings and curses. Now choose life, so that you and your children may live"*

2. Joshua 24:15 *"But if serving the LORD seems undesirable to you, then choose for yourselves this day whom you will serve, whether the gods your ancestors served beyond the Euphrates, or the gods of the Amorites, in whose land you are living. But as for me and my household, we will serve the LORD."* Joshua does indicate that man has a choice in choosing God. However, what rational person would choose death and curses over life and blessings.

Bible Verses that Support "Limited Freewill"

The assumption is that those who turned away from faith/belief in Christ received the   Holy Spirit and were saved but later turned away from their faith:

1. John 6:60 *"On hearing it, many of his disciples said, "This is a hard teaching Who can accept it?" Afterward many disciples left Jesus."*

2. Matthew 24:*24* *"For false messiahs and false prophets will appear and perform great signs and wonders to deceive, if possible, even the elect."*

3. Hebrews 10:26-27 *"If we deliberately keep on sinning after we have received the knowledge of the truth, no sacrifice for sins is left, *[27]* but only a fearful expectation of judgment and of raging fire that will consume the enemies of God."*

4. 4. Hebrews 6:4-6 *"It is impossible for those who have once been enlightened, who have tasted the heavenly gift, who have shared in the Holy Spirit, *[5]* who have tasted*

> *the goodness of the word of God and the powers of the coming age* [6] *and who have fallen away, to be brought back to repentance. To their loss they are crucifying the Son of God all over again and subjecting him to public disgrace."*

5. Peter 2:20 *"If they have escaped the corruption of the world by knowing our Lord and Savior Jesus Christ and are again entangled in it and are overcome, they are worse off at the end than they were at the beginning."*

There are good arguments on both sides of the issue. Belief in "forever saved" or "apostasy" has nothing to do with weather or not you are saved. Only faith/belief in Jesus Christ as Lord and Savior will accomplish that. Since neither view has anything to do with one's salvation, disagreement by denominations causes dissention among the churches and gives Satan a foothold. Satan the accuser thrives on division!

Bible Verses that Support "One Work" or "Once Saved Forever Saved"

A division among different protestant denominations is in regard to the permanence of man's salvation. Those churches that teach "decisions theology" and "limited free will" believe that after you have been saved that you can later apostasy or fall away. Judas, one of Jesus' original twelve disciples may be an example of apostasy.

The "one work" churches teach that once you are saved, you can never lose your salvation. They believe that Judas or any other apostate person never truly believed Following are Bible verses that support the "one work" of forever saved belief:

1. John 10:28 *"I give them eternal life, and they shall never perish; no one will snatch them out of my hand.* [29] *My*

Father, who has given them to me, is greater than all; no one can snatch them out of my Father's hand."

2. John 6:39-40 *"And this is the will of him who sent me, that I shall lose none of all those he has given me, but raise them up at the last day. [40] For my Father's will is that everyone who looks to the Son and believes in him shall have eternal life, and I will raise them up at the last day."*

3. John 17:2 *"For you granted him authority over all people that he might give eternal life to all those you have given him."* Note that Jesus says "all" and seems to imply only those given Jesus by the Father..

4. John 17:24 *"Father, I want those you have given me to be with me where I am, and to see my glory, the glory you have given me because you loved me before the creation of the world."* Would God deny His son's request?

5. Romans 11:29 *"for God's gifts and his call are irrevocable."*

All the Credit for Your Salvation is God's

We are told to let the Bible interrupt itself by finding clearer passages to understand less clear passages. According to *"Strong's Concise Concordance of the Bible"*, freewill is mentioned only 17 times and all refer to "freewill offerings" not freewill to chose God. Variations of the words chosen, election and predestination are mentioned 238 times. When you include "called" and "appointed" which in many instances have similar meanings with chosen, there are just too many times to count. Following is the breakdown by variations of the words:

1. Chosen = 210 times
2. Election = 24 times
3. Predestined = 4 times
4. Called and Appointed = too many count

We are free to make every day decisions which involve choosing sins he/she will commit. However, God's people are chosen in spite of their sins, not because they are better, smarter or less sinful than someone else: John 15:16 *"You did not choose me, but I chose you and appointed you to go and bear fruit—fruit that will last. Then the Father will give you whatever you ask in my name."* The fruit that will last is the good works we do for God. If you have doubts about this concept, be like the Bereans and check this out for yourself.

Man is Not to Judge God's Choices

It is not up to man to judge God's choices or motives. Matthew 7:1-5 *"Do not judge, or you too will be judged. [2] For in the same way you judge others, you will be judged, and with the measure you use, it will be measured to you.[3] "Why do you look at the speck of sawdust in your brother's eye and pay no attention to the plank in your own eye?[4] How can you say to your brother, 'Let me take the speck out of your eye,' when all the time there is a plank in your own eye?[5] You hypocrite, first take the plank out of your own eye, and then you will see clearly to remove the speck from your brother's eye.* It is so much easier to see our neighbor's sins than our own sins. God is the judge of man's sins not man!

Who are we to question the creator of the universe? Romans 9:20-21 *"But who are you, O man, to talk back to God?" Shall what is formed say to him who formed it, 'Why did you make me like this?"[21]Does not the potter have the right to make out of the same lump of clay some pottery for noble purposes and some for common use?*

Those that are born again through God's Spirit should be eternally grateful, not judgmental! 2 Thessalonians 2:13-14 *"But we ought always to thank God for you, brothers and sisters loved by the Lord, because God chose you as firstfruits to be saved through the sanctifying work of the Spirit and through belief in the truth.[14] He called you to this through our gospel that you might share in the glory of our Lord Jesus Christ."*

God chooses to save some people, not because they were better, smarter, less sinful or more deserving than others, but because God is God and we are not!

How Can I know if I am one of God's Children?

Believe in the following:

1. That there is only one true God and He created everything out of nothing.

2. That Jesus Christ is the "One and Only Son of God" and that He died, he was buried and rose from the dead.

3. That Jesus paid in full the price for all your sins; past, present and future through His sacrifice on the cross and is the only way to receive eternal life in Heaven.

4. That salvation is a "gift" from God and I can never be "good" enough to earn my salvation.

5. That although I will fail, I am no longer a slave to sin and will do my best to keep God's commandments.

6. That when I sin, I will repent and pray for God's forgiveness.

7. That I will continue to grow in my faith by studying God's Word.

8. That because of the Holy Spirit in me, I am a new and changed person that is not afraid of proclaiming to be a follower of Christ.

If you believe all the above you will help share the "Good News" of Jesus Christ with others so they may spend eternity in Heaven as a child of God. If you don't believe that Jesus is God and He died for all your, you will spend eternity separated from God in Hell.

1. <u>Mark 16:16</u> *"Whoever believes and is baptized will be saved, but whoever does not believe will be condemned."*

2. <u>John 3:36</u> *"Whoever believes in the Son has eternal life, but whoever rejects the Son will not see life, for God's wrath remains on him."*

3. <u>John 8:24</u> *"I told you that you would die in your sins; if you do not believe that I am the one I claim to be, you will indeed die in your sins."*

Why Bother to Promote the Gospel?

Reason why we should share God's Good News:

1. God commanded us to: <u>Matthew 28:19-20</u> *"Therefore go and make disciples of all nations, baptizing them in the name of the Father and of the Son and of the Holy Spirit, [20] and teaching them to obey everything I have commanded you. And surely I am with you always, to the very end of the age."*

2. We don't know who God's children are: <u>Matthew 7:1</u> *"Do not judge, or you too will be judged."* Some people may go for many years before God's Holy Spirit comes upon them. However, who knows when seeds that were sowed by someone years ago will take root. The thief on the cross was saved just shortly before he died.

3. Just because God does the choosing, He still requires believers to carry his message: <u>Romans 10:15</u> *"And how can they preach unless they are sent? As it is written, "How beautiful are the feet of those who bring good news!"*

4. The Holy Spirit will help and give us the words to say. <u>Romans 8:26-27</u> *"In the same way, the Spirit helps us in our weakness. We do not know what we ought to pray*

for, but the Spirit himself intercedes for us with groans that words cannot express. ²⁷And he who searches our hearts knows the mind of the Spirit, because the Spirit intercedes for the saints in accordance with God's will."

Conclusion:

Without God's Holy Spirit sinful man would not seek God or be able to understand Him. Satan's followers are people that God does not want to know His message of salvation. Luke 8:10 *"He said, "The knowledge of the secrets of the kingdom of God has been given to you, but to others I speak in parables, so that, '"though seeing, they may not see; though hearing, they may not understand.'"*

God's Word contains dozens of clear bible passages relating to freewill in this chapter. It is God who chooses who will accept His gift of faith and spend eternity with Him. Ephesians 1:13-14 *"And you also were included in Christ when you heard the message of truth, the gospel of your salvation. When you believed, you were marked in him with a seal, the promised Holy Spirit, ¹⁴ who is a deposit guaranteeing our inheritance until the redemption of those who are God's possession—to the praise of his glory."* Belief/faith is the key to salvation and without the Holy Spirit, the Gospel is foolishness and veiled to those who are perishing.

Satan will encourage anything that diminishes God. Satan attempts to builds up man's ego by have him take credit for all his blessings. It doesn't take much to convince man that through their own intelligence they are in control of their salvation. This myth fits nicely into man's prideful ego and takes away the sovereignty of God.

Having people believe that man has freewill to choose Christ, makes the church essential in in making a decision for Christ. The church is very important in getting out the strengthening ones faith, but salvation is all up to God!.

Since we were all born spiritually dead, it does not matter how much water or fertilizer a dead seed receives, it is only through God's gift of His Holy Spirit that brings some dead seeds to spiritual life. God's chosen, called, elect, appointed or predestined are

His children and He helps them grow through miraculous spiritual re birth. "There by the grace of God go I". Salvation = 100% God + 0% man!

CHAPTER 5

THE TRUTH WILL SET YOU FREE

Myth # 3: God Loves Everyone Unconditionally

Unconditional love vs. God's Wrath

Does God love antichrists and those who are in Hell eternally with no chance of repentances unconditionally? The concept that God loves everyone regardless how they live/lived their lives is not Biblical. Over 2500 years ago the false prophets in Israel were claiming that because they were descendants of Abraham, God wasn't concerned about their behavior. The religious leaders ignored God's true prophets like Isaiah and Jeremiah who foretold of God's coming wrath. Foolishly they believed that God's wrath was only directed toward the heathen Gentiles.

Love according to Paul: 1 Corinthians 13:4-7 *"Love is patient, love is kind. It does not envy, it does not boast, it is not proud. [5] It is not rude, it is not self-seeking, it is not easily angered, it keeps no record of wrongs. [6] Love does not delight in evil but rejoices with the truth. [7] It always protects, always trusts, always hopes, always perseveres."*

Many pastors/priests separate salvation/eternal life from God's unconditional love for all mankind. They take only a portion of the Gospel of John as proof that God loves everyone unconditionally. John 3:16 *"For God so loved the world that He gave His one and only son"* This leads many people to believe that God loves:

- Those who deny the very existence of a God
- Unrepentant sinner.
- Those who deny Jesus' sacrifice on the cross for the forgiveness of their sins.

However, John goes on to say:

1. John 3:16 *whoever believes in him shall not perish but have eternal life.* Isn't belief in Jesus a condition of eternal life? The Bible is very clear that there are conditions for one's salvation: faith/belief, repentance, loving God, and forgiving others.

2. John 3:18 *"Whoever believes in him is not condemned, but whoever does not believe stands condemned already because they have not believed in the name of God's one and only Son.*

3. John 3:36 *"Whoever believes in the Son has eternal life, but whoever rejects the Son will not see life, for God's wrath remains on them."* Without faith /belief you will suffer God's wrath and die in your sins!

4. John 8:4 *"Yet because I tell the truth, you do not believe me!"*

5. John 8:24 *"I told you that you would die in your sins; if you do not believe that I am he, you will indeed die in your sins."* Hell is where the lost will live when they die where there will be weeping and gnashing of teeth as punishment for all their unrepentant sins.

An excerpt from *God's Love* by R.C. Sproul published by David C

<u>Cook</u> states: *It has become fashionable in evangelical circles to speak somewhat glibly of the unconditional love of God. It is certainly a pleasing message for people to hear and conforms to a certain kind of political correctness. In our desire to communicate to people the sweetness of the gospel, the readiness of God to cover our sins with forgiveness, and the incredible depth of His love displayed on the cross, we indulge in a hyperbolic expression of the scope and extent of His love.*

Where in Scripture do we find this notion of the unconditional love of God? If God's love is absolutely unconditional, why do we tell people that they have to repent and have faith in order to be saved? God sets forth clear conditions for a person to be saved. It may be true that in some sense God loves even those who fail to meet the conditions of salvation, but that subtlety is often missed by the hearer when the preacher declares the unconditional love of God. People hear that God will continue to love them and accept them, no matter what they do or how they live. We might as well declare an unabashed universalism as to declare the unconditional love of God without a clear and careful qualification of what that means ".

<u>Dr. Sproul</u> goes on to say: *His sacrifice was not designed to satisfy our unjust enmity toward God but to satisfy God's just wrath toward us. The Father was the object of the Son's act of propitiation. The effect of the cross was to remove the divine estrangement from us, not our estrangement from Him. If we deny God's estrangement from us, the cross is reduced to a pathetic and anemic moral influence with no substitutionary satisfaction of God".*

Did God Love These People Unconditionally?

Did God love the whole world unconditionally when every person and creature except righteous Noah and his family were destroyed during the great flood? <u>Genesis 6:13</u> *"So God said to Noah, "I am going to put an end to all people, for the earth is filled with violence because of them. I am surely going to destroy both them and the earth."*

Did God love everyone when He destroyed all but 6 people in Sodom and Gomorra? Genesis 19:24-25 *"Then the LORD rained down burning sulfur on Sodom and Gomorrah—from the LORD out of the heavens.²⁵ Thus he overthrew those cities and the entire plain, destroying all those living in the cities—and also the vegetation in the land."*

Did God love every first born male in Egypt when He killed them and freed the Israelites? Exodus 12:12 *"On that same night I will pass through Egypt and strike down every firstborn of both people and animals, and I will bring judgment on all the gods of Egypt. I am the LORD. "*

Did God love everyone unconditionally when He had the Israelites kill every man, woman and child when conquering the "Promised Land"? 1 Samuel 15:3 *"Now go, attack the Amalekites and totally destroy all that belongs to them. Do not spare them; put to death men and women, children and infants, cattle and sheep, camels and donkeys.'"*

Did God Love "This People" Unconditionally?

1. Luke 21:23 *"How dreadful it will be in those days for pregnant women and nursing mothers! There will be great distress in the land and wrath against this people."*

2. Jeremiah 7:33 *"Then the carcasses of this people will become food for the birds and the wild animals, and there will be no one to frighten them away."*

3. Jeremiah 7:16 *"So do not pray for this people nor offer any plea or petition for them; do not plead with me, for I will not listen to you."*

4. Isaiah was sent to tell "*this people*" that they there cities would lie ruined and without inhabitants, their fields would be ruined and ravaged and the land utterly forsaken. Isaiah 6:11-12 *"Then I said, "For how long, Lord?" And*

he answered: "Until the cities lie ruined and without inhabitant, until the houses are left deserted and the fields ruined and ravaged, ¹² until the LORD has sent everyone far away and the land is utterly forsaken."

What Does "Unconditionally" Mean?

Webster defines "unconditional": *"not limited in any way"* and *"unconditioned"*: *"not subject to conditions."* You will not find any mention of "unconditional love" in the Bible! However, qualifiers or conditions such as "if you", whoever", "all who", "he who does what is right" etc. are used numerous times in the Bible making an unconditional statement conditional.

1. Obedience to God's commands, loving Him, and forgiveness of others, are conditions for God's blessings/love throughout the Bible.

2. In the New Testament, after Christ's sacrifice on the cross for sinful man, faith/ belief in Jesus became a condition of salvation and eternal life today.

How many times have you heard that "God loves everyone unconditionally"? This is another myth that Satan uses to confuse man and create doubt as to the truth of the Bible. Doubting something is the opposite of faith. Believing you are loved unconditionally gives you the false belief that God doesn't care about your sins. Doubting God's word and not being concerned about sin is the broad path that leads to destruction! Matthew 7:21 *"Not everyone who says to me, 'Lord, Lord,' will enter the kingdom of heaven, but only the one who does the will of my Father who is in heaven."* Trusting God and doing His will, being obedient", are condition of God's love.

Why is Belief in God's Unconditional Love Dangerous?

God gave us both LAW and GOSPEL for a reason. Focusing just on / God's love, is illogical, confusing, non-Biblical and dangerous!

1. <u>Illogical</u> – God loving everyone unconditional implies that He doesn't care how you live your life, weather you deny Him and Jesus, weather you hate your brother, hold grudges against those who hurt you, that you love evil, etc. Does God really love those who follow the evil mentioned above? If so, why are they sent to Hell, a place of eternal torment with no chance of redemption? That doesn't make since to a logical person.

2. <u>Confusing</u> – Does world history show any evidence that God loves "everyone" unconditionally? Why would a loving God allow: wars, natural disasters, disease and personal loss of a love one occur? If God is all-powerful and in control of everything why would He allow these things to happen? These events make many people either doubt God's love for mankind and/or His power over these events.

3. <u>Un–Biblical</u> – Nowhere in the Bible does God offer salvation without the condition of belief and or faith. In fact it takes away one of God's powerful tools, the fear of His wrath, in order to get people to seek after Him. <u>Psalm 111:10</u> ***"The fear of the Lord is the beginning of knowledge; all who follow his precepts have good understanding."*** <u>Proverbs 1:7</u> ***"The fear of the Lord is the beginning of knowledge, but fools despise wisdom and discipline."*** <u>Revelation 14:7</u> ***"He said in a loud voice, "Fear God and give him glory, because the hour of his judgment has come. Worship him who made the heavens, the earth, the sea and the springs of water."*** <u>2 Chronicles 19:7</u> ***"Now let the fear of the lord be upon you. Judge carefully for, with the Lord***

our God there is no injustice or partiality or bribery." Satan is delighted when sinners don't fear God!

4. <u>Dangerous</u> – It gives Satan ammunition to dispute God's word and convince doubting Christians that the Bible is not accurate. Satan has been successful in getting many Christian churches, in order to gain/keep members, to compromise God's Word on many issues like gay marriage, abortion and homosexuality. These miss-guided churches have diluted God's message by promising blessings through financial giving and church attendance. They fail to talk about man's greatest problem, sin.

What is the Purpose of the Law?

The "Law" was given to man thousands of years before the Gospel for a reason. Unforgiven sin or disobedience to God's" law" was/is the cause of death of all life on earth. God is a God of love for all His chosen believers, but He is also a God of "wrath" for unbelievers, the children of Satan. Because unbelievers don't accept Jesus' shed blood on the cross as payment in full for all their sins, they must pay sin's penalty themselves.

Unbelief results in God's wrath, condemnation and death. <u>Webster's Dictionary</u> defines **"wrath"**: *"violent anger: RAGE"*, God's wrath falls on all unrepentant sinners, those who deny God the creator and Jesus' sacrifice on the cross.

Assuming that you desire to know the "truth" you must put your trust in what the Bible actually says rather in what you have heard or what you feel is correct. There is no question that God is a God of love but God also is a God of wrath because He hates sin. The Bible also says that God is just, omniscient, omnipotent, omnipresent and sovereign. God exercises His sovereignty! <u>Romans 9:15</u> *"For he says to Moses, "I will have mercy on whom I have mercy, and I will have compassion on whom I have compassion."*

God does not love those who try and destroy the relationship that

God intended for man before sin came into the world. That is why God created Hell for Satan and his followers. God is a God of love for all His chosen believers, but He is also a God of "wrath" for unbelievers, the children of Satan. Because unbelievers don't accept Jesus' shed blood on the cross as payment in full for all their sins, they must pay sin's penalty themselves.

In the Old Testament God struck down those who worshiped other gods.

1. Exodus 32:33-35: *"The Lord replied to Moses, "Whoever has sinned against me I will blot out of my book. [34] Now go, lead the people to the place I spoke of and my angel will go before you. However, when the time comes for me to punish, I will punish them for their sin." And the Lord struck the people with a plague because of what they did with the calf Aaron had made."*_

2. Exodus 20:3-6: *"You shall have no other gods before me. [4]"You shall not make for yourself an image in the form of anything in heaven above or on the earth beneath or in the waters below. [5] You shall not bow down to them or worship them; for I, the LORD your God, am a jealous God, punishing the children for the sin of the parents to the third and fourth generation of those who hate me, [6] but showing love to a thousand generations of those who love me and keep my commandments."* God is a jealous God and will not tolerate idol worship or anything that comes before Him. That includes family, money, power etc.

3. Deuteronomy 7:9-10: *"Know therefore that the LORD your God is God; he is the faithful God, keeping his covenant of love to a thousand generations of those who love him and keep his commandments. [10] But those who hate him he will repay to their face by destruction; he will not be slow to repay to their face those who hate him."*

4. Deuteronomy 11:13: *"So if you faithfully obey the*

commands I am giving you today—to love the Lord your God and to serve him with all your heart and with all your soul— [14] *then I will send rain on your land in its season, both autumn and spring rains, so that you may gather in your grain, new wine and olive oil."*

5. Deuteronomy 11:22": *"If you carefully observe all these commands I am giving you to follow—to love the Lord your God, to walk in obedience to him and to hold fast to him—* [23] *then the Lord will drive out all these nations before you, and you will dispossess nations larger and stronger than you."*

6. Deuteronomy 11:27-28: *"the blessing if you obey the commands of the LORD your God that I am giving you today;* [28] *the curse if you disobey the commands of the LORD your God and turn from the way that I command you today by following other gods, which you have not known.".*

7. Deuteronomy 30:17-18: *" But if your heart turns away and you are not obedient, and if you are drawn away to bow down to other gods and worship them,* [18] *I declare to you this day that you will certainly be destroyed. You will not live long in the land you are crossing the Jordan to enter and possess."*

8. Deuteronomy 32:41: *"when I sharpen my flashing sword and my hand grasps it in judgment, I will take vengeance on my adversaries and repay those who hate me.*

9. 2 Chronicles 19:2 *"Should you help the wicked and love those who hate the Lord? Because of this, the wrath of the Lord is on you."*

10. Psalm5:5-6: *"The arrogant cannot stand in your presence; you hate all who do wrong.* [6] *You destroy those who tell lies; bloodthirsty and deceitful men the LORD abhors."* God hasn't changed His mind on these sins today.

11. Psalm 7:11: "*God is a righteous judge, a God who expresses his wrath every day.*" Can God love everyone and also be a God of Wrath?

12. Psalm 11:5-6: "*The LORD examines the righteous, but the wicked and those who love violence his soul hates. ⁶ On the wicked he will rain fiery coals and burning sulfur; a scorching wind will be their lot.*" Dose God love the wicked unconditionally?

13. Psalms 25:10: "*All the ways of the LORD are loving and faithful for those who keep the demands of his covenant.*" Isn't, "for those who keep the demands of his covenant" a condition?

14. Psalm 45:7: "*You love righteousness and hate wickedness*"

15. Psalm 60:5: "*Save us and help us with your right hand, that those you love may be delivered.*"

16. Psalm 71:27: "*Those who are far from you will perish; you destroy all who are unfaithful to you.*" Here faithfulness is a condition.

17. Psalm 73:27: "*Those who are far from you will perish; you destroy all who are unfaithful to you.*"

18. Psalm 78:62: "*He gave his people over to the sword; he was furious with his inheritance.*" Is this unconditional love?

19. Psalm 94:23: "*He will repay them for their sins and destroy them for their wickedness; the LORD our God will destroy them.*" Is this unconditional love?

20. Psalm 103:17: "*But from everlasting to everlasting the LORD's love is with those who fear him, and his righteousness with their children's children*" Is fear a condition?

21. Psalm 145:20: "*The LORD watches over all who love him, but all the wicked he will destroy.*"

22. <u>Proverbs 8:13:</u> *"To fear the Lord is to hate evil; I hate pride and arrogance, evil behavior and perverse speech."*

23. <u>Proverbs 11:20-21:</u> *"The Lord detests those whose hearts are perverse but delights in those whose ways are blameless. 21 Be sure of this: The wicked will not go unpunished, but those who are righteous will go free."*

24. <u>Ecclesiastes 3:8:</u> *"a time to love and a time to hate, a time for war and a time for peace."*

25. <u>Isaiah 61:8:</u> *"For I, the LORD, love justice; I hate robbery and iniquity. In my faithfulness I will reward them and make an everlasting covenant with them."*

26. <u>Isaiah 63:3:</u> *"I have trodden the winepress alone; from the nations no one was with me. I trampled them in my anger and trod them down in my wrath; their blood spattered my garments, and I stained all my clothing.*

27. <u>Daniel 9:4:</u> *"Lord, the great and awesome God, who keeps his covenant of love with those who love him and keep his commandments,*

28. <u>Malachi 1:3:</u> *"but Esau I have hated, and I have turned his mountains into a wasteland and left his inheritance to the desert jackals."*

Conditions for God's Love in the New Testament

1. <u>Matthew 6:14-15:</u> *"For if you forgive other people when they sin against you, your heavenly Father will also forgive you. 15 But if you do not forgive others their sins, your Father will not forgive your sins.*

2. <u>Matthew 18:34-35:</u> *"In anger his master handed him over to the jailers to be tortured, until he should pay back all he owed.35 "This is how my heavenly Father will treat*

each of you unless you forgive your brother or sister from your heart."

3. Matthew 24:51: *"He will cut him to pieces and assign him a place with the hypocrites, where there will be weeping and gnashing of teeth."*

4. Matthew 7:19: *"Every tree that does not bear good fruit is cut down and thrown into the fire.* Bearing good fruit is a condition for salvation.

5. Matthew 26:41,46: *"Then he will say to those on his left, 'Depart from me, you who are cursed, into the eternal fire prepared for the devil and his angels"....* [46] *"Then they will go away to eternal punishment, but the righteous to eternal life."*

6. Luke 13:3,5: *"I tell you, no! But unless you repent, you too will all perish."* Note this is repeated twice for importance!

7. Romans 2:5-8: *"But because of your stubbornness and your unrepentant heart, you are storing up wrath against yourself for the day of God's wrath, when his righteous judgment will be revealed.* [6] *God "will repay each person according to what they have done."* [7] *To those who by persistence in doing good seek glory, honor and immortality, he will give eternal life.* [8] *But for those who are self-seeking and who reject the truth and follow evil, there will be wrath and anger."*

8. Romans 2:13: *"For it is not those who hear the law who are righteous in God's sight, but it is those who obey the law who will be declared righteous.* Obedience is a condition of righteousness or salvation.

9. Ephesians 1:13: *"And you also were included in Christ when you heard the message of truth, the gospel of your salvation. When you believed, you were marked in him with a seal, the promised Holy Spirit"* Again, belief.

10. Ephesians 5:6: *"Let no one deceive you with empty words, for because of such things God's wrath comes on those who are disobedient."*

11. Hebrews 5:9: *"and, once made perfect, he became the source of eternal salvation for all who obey him"* Again, conditional on obedience.

12. 1 Peter 3:12: *"For the eyes of the Lord are on the righteous and his ears are attentive to their prayers, but the face of the Lord is against those who do evil."*

13. Revelation 14:9-10: *"A third angel followed them and said in a loud voice: "If anyone worships the beast and its image and receives its mark on their forehead or on their hand, [10] they, too, will drink the wine of God's fury, which has been poured full strength into the cup of his wrath. They will be tormented with burning sulfur in the presence of the holy angels and of the Lamb."*

14. Revelation 14:19-: *"The angel swung his sickle on the earth, gathered its grapes and threw them into the great winepress of God's wrath. [20] They were trampled in the winepress outside the city, and blood flowed out of the press, rising as high as the horses' bridles for a distance of 1,600 stadia".*

15. Revelation 18:1-8: *Give her as much torment and grief as the glory and luxury she gave herself. "In her heart she boasts, 'I sit enthroned as queen. I am not a widow; I will never mourn. [8] Therefore in one day her plagues will overtake her: death, mourning and famine. She will be consumed by fire, for mighty is the Lord God who judges her."*

Does any of this sound like unconditional love?

Satan Loves to Create Doubts about God's Word

God doesn't cause horrific things to happen, but He does allow them to happen. Man is held accountable for both sins of omission, sins that we commit because we refuse to do something that we know we ought to do as well as sins of commission, sins caused by breaking one of God's commandments. I believe God allows horrific things to happen because:

1. God disciplines His children just as loving parents discipline their children wen they get out of line.

2. Eternal life is something everyone will experience; however the location of where you spend eternity matters immensely! For God's saved, believers, it matters little how long he/she spends here on earth. Heaven is far superior to life on earth.

3. We grow closer to God in times of trouble than when everything is going smoothly. Pride enters in and turns us away from God and taking credit for all our successes.

4. Difficult experiences that we survive help us have compassion on others suffering from a similar experience.

What difference does it make if a Saint/believer is killed at a young age and goes directly to Heaven rather than spending more time on earth? On the other hand if you deny Christ and die, you will go to Hell early for eternity. Yes, the loss will affect loved ones on earth for a time, but life on earth it is a drop in the ocean when compared to eternity.

Does God love Those in Hell?

I don't believe that God loves the people that go to Hell for eternity, with a fire that never can be quenched. Hell is eternal suffering with no chance of a repentance, pardon or release. God created Hell for the unrighteous, the ungodly, the unrepentant and all who deny Him Jesus.

God created Heaven for all His children, those who believe in Him and Jesus's shed blood on the cross for the forgiveness of all their sins.

1. John 8:24 *"I told you that you would die in your sins; if you do not believe that I am he, you will indeed die in your sins."* Dying in your sins is spending eternity in Hell!

2. Jude 1:5 *"Though you already know all this, I want to remind you that the Lord at one time delivered his people out of Egypt, but later destroyed those who did not believe."* Faith or belief in God/Jesus is the only way to escape condemnation and eternal damnation.

3. 2 Peter 2:4-9 *"For if God did not spare angels when they sinned, but sent them to hell, putting them in chains of darkness to be held for judgment; ^{5} if he did not spare the ancient world when he brought the flood on its ungodly people, but protected Noah, a preacher of righteousness, and seven others; ^{6} if he condemned the cities of Sodom and Gomorrah by burning them to ashes, and made them an example of what is going to happen to the ungodly; ^{7} and if he rescued Lot, a righteous man, who was distressed by the depraved conduct of the lawless ^{8} (for that righteous man, living among them day after day, was tormented in his righteous soul by the lawless deeds he saw and heard)— ^{9} if this is so, then the Lord knows how to rescue the godly from trials and to hold the unrighteous for punishment on the day of judgment."* Psalm 135:10-12 *"He struck down many nations and killed mighty kings- 11 Sihon king of the Amorites, Og king of Bashan and all the kings of Canaan- 12 and he gave their land as an inheritance, an inheritance to his people Israel."* Here God took land away from other nations and gave it to" His chosen people".

4. Deuteronomy 7:1-2 *"When the LORD your God brings you into the land you are entering to possess and drives*

out before you many nations—the Hittites, Girgashites, Amorites, Canaanites, Perizzites, Hivites and Jebusites, seven nations larger and stronger than you- [2] *and when the LORD your God has delivered them over to you and you have defeated them, then you must destroy them totally. Make no treaty with them, and show them no mercy."* Totally destroying all the above people and showing them no mercy is a far cry from unconditional love!_

5. Isaiah 49:26 *"I will make your oppressors eat their own flesh; they will be drunk on their own blood, as with wine. Then all mankind will know that I, the LORD, am your Savior, your Redeemer, the Mighty One of Jacob."* Did God love Israel's oppressors?

Does God Love Satan and His Children?

I am not questioning God's unconditional love for believers or "His children". God knows who His children are and who Satan's children are by their actions and hate toward their neighbors.. 1 John 3:10 *"This is how we know who the children of God are and who the children of the devil are: Anyone who does not do what is right is not God's child, nor is anyone who does not love their brother and sister.* You can't fool God for He knows the heart of man and clearly distinguishes His children from Satan and children. Call it predestination or foreknowledge, no one can deceive God. Would God give up His one and only Son to suffer and die for someone that He knew would reject His gift of Salvation?

God loves the world so much that He made a way for "His" children, believers, to have an eternal relationship with Him even though they had committed numerous sins. In God's time all people will be judged. Matthew 14:49-50 *"This is how it will be at the end of the age. The angels will come and separate the wicked from the righteous* [50] *and throw them into the blazing furnace, where there will be weeping and gnashing of teeth."* Satan's children are destined to stumble over

Christ the "Capstone". <u>1 Peter 2:8</u> " *and, "A stone that causes people to stumble and a rock that makes them fall."* They stumble because they disobey the message—which is also what they were destined for."* God knows who will stumble and their eternal destiny.

The Bible says that God is love' therefore that is absolutely true:

1. <u>Psalm 57:10</u> *"For great is your love, reaching to the heavens; your faithfulness reaches to the skies."* This doesn't say He loves everyone.

2. <u>Psalm 108:4</u> *"For great is your love, higher than the heavens; your faithfulness reaches to the skies."* This love is for His children, believers.

3. <u>Psalm 107:21</u> *"Let them give thanks to the LORD for his unfailing love and his wonderful deeds for men."*

However, Jesus makes it clear what happens to unbelievers who don't accept Him as King in the "parable of the 10 minas" Jesus says: <u>Luke 19:27</u> *"But those enemies of mine who did not want me to be king over them—bring them here and kill them in front of me."* Jesus is talking about Satan's children, unbelievers, who Jesus wants killed because they refused to accept Him as their King.

God's Chosen People

God's chosen people were given clear instructions about idol worship, and followed their own desires. <u>Isaiah 43:10-11</u> *"You are my witnesses,"* *declares the LORD, "and my servant whom I have chosen, so that you may know and believe me and understand that I am he. Before me no god was formed, nor will there be one after me. [11] I, even I, am the LORD, and apart from me there is no savior."* Isaiah was talking about a future Messiah, Jesus, who would become the world's only savior

In spite of all that God had done for Israel most of their people preferred having a worldly king. They were involved in intercourse with temple prostitutes, drunken orgies etc. rather than worshiping the Lord who rescued them from slavery in Egypt! Romans 21-28 *"For although they knew God, they neither glorified him as God nor gave thanks to him, but their thinking became futile and their foolish hearts were darkened. ²² Although they claimed to be wise, they became fools ²³ and exchanged the glory of the immortal God for images made to look like a mortal human being and birds and animals and reptiles. ²⁴ Therefore God gave them over in the sinful desires of their hearts to sexual impurity for the degrading of their bodies with one another. ²⁵ They exchanged the truth about God for a lie, and worshiped and served created things rather than the Creator—who is forever praised. Amen. ²⁶ Because of this, God gave them over to shameful lusts. Even their women exchanged natural sexual relations for unnatural ones. ²⁷ In the same way the men also abandoned natural relations with women and were inflamed with lust for one another. Men committed shameful acts with other men, and received in themselves the due penalty for their error. ²⁸ Furthermore, just as they did not think it worthwhile to retain the knowledge of God, so God gave them over to a depraved mind, so that they do what ought not to be done."* Paul goes on to say: Romans 1:31 *"Although they know God's righteous decree that those who do such things deserve death, they not only continue to do these very things but also approve of those who practice them."* God's wrath against sexual shameful lusts for one another hasn't changed over the last two thousand years. Man's approval of this deviant sexual behavior of others has grown despite God's severe warnings.

God is just and punishes those who reject His ways. Isaiah 42:24 *"Who handed Jacob over to become loot, and Israel to the plunderers? Was it not the LORD, against whom we have sinned? For they would not follow his ways; they did not obey his law. ²⁵ So he poured out on them his burning anger, the violence of war. It enveloped them in flames, yet they did not understand; it consumed them, but they did not take it to heart."*

Even today the Jews are still suffering from their rejection of Jesus. Some day they will be brought back into His family and they will accept

Jesus as their Lord and savior. Gentiles were grafted into God's chosen family tree in order to make the Jews, His chosen people envious"

1. Romans 11:11 *"Again I ask: Did they stumble so as to fall beyond recovery? Not at all! Rather, because of their transgression, salvation has come to the Gentiles to make Israel envious."*

2. Romans 11:19-21 *"You will say then, "Branches were broken off so that I could be grafted in."* [20] *Granted. But they were broken off because of unbelief, and you stand by faith. Do not be arrogant, but tremble.* [21] *For if God did not spare the natural branches, he will not spare you either."* God is just therefore He detests and punishes sin!

Most parents love their children regardless of what they do and try to teach them right from wrong. Loving Christian parents will continue to discipline/teach their children Christian values as long as they live. After they are grown and responsible for their actions they will keep trying to change any bad/criminal behavior.

Today many professing Christians don't worship the God of the Bible, instead worship a god of their own creation. It is much easier to worship a liberal god we create rather than the just "wrathful" God of the Bible. Loving anyone or anything more than God is idol worship.

God dearly loves His chosen, His elect, called, appointed and those He predestined before the foundation of the world unconditionally. Colossians 3:12 *"Therefore, as God's chosen people, holy and dearly loved, clothe yourselves with compassion, kindness, humility, gentleness and patience."* Are the above traits suggestions or commands?

Does God Want Everyone to Understand His Message of Salvation?

There are some people God does not want to understand His message of salvation. If God loves everyone unconditionally and desires all to come to repentance, why would He prevent some people from turning from their sinful ways and be healed? How can God love "all people unconditionally" when He blinds the eyes of unbelievers so they won't accept the Gospel message? Following are verses that exclude people from hearing/understanding God's message of salvation:

1. Matthew 11:25 *"At that time Jesus said, "I praise you, Father, Lord of heaven and earth, because you have hidden these things from the wise and learned, and revealed them to little children.*

2. Matthew 13:11 *"He replied, "The knowledge of the secrets of the kingdom of heaven has been given to you, but not to them."* If God loves everyone, why keep the secrets of the kingdom of heaven from anyone?

3. Matthew 13:13 Jesus said: *"This is why I speak to them in parables: "Though seeing, they do not see; though hearing, they do not hear or understand."* Jesus repeats Isaiah's quote from the Old Testament.

4. Matthew 13:14-15 *"In them is fulfilled the prophecy of Isaiah: "'You will be ever hearing but never understanding; you will be ever seeing but never perceiving.* [15] *For this people's heart has become calloused; they hardly hear with their ears, and they have closed their eyes. Otherwise they might see with their eyes, hear with their ears, understand with their hearts and turn, and I would heal them."*

5. Luke 8:9 *"His disciples asked him what this parable meant.* [10] *He said, "The knowledge of the secrets of the kingdom of God has been given to you, but to others I speak in parables, so that, "'though seeing, they may not see; though hearing, they may not understand."*

6. 1 Corinthians 1: 19 *"For it is written: "I will destroy the*

wisdom of the wise; the intelligence of the intelligent I will frustrate."

7. <u>1 Corinthians 1:27</u> *"But God chose the foolish things of the world to shame the wise; God chose the weak things of the world to shame the strong".* It is prideful to believe that we could actually make a choice for Jesus through our own intelligence, and God hates pride.

8. <u>2 Corinthians 4:3-4</u> *"And even if our gospel is veiled, it is veiled to those who are perishing. ⁴ The god of this age has blinded the minds of unbelievers, so that they cannot see the light of the gospel that displays the glory of Christ, who is the image of God."* Again, why keep the gospel message from anyone if you loved them?

9. <u>Isaiah 6:9</u> *He said, "Go and tell this people: "'Be ever hearing, but never understanding; be ever seeing, but never perceiving.'¹⁰ Make the heart of this people calloused; make their ears dull and close their eyes, Otherwise they might see with their eyes, hear with their ears, understand with their hearts, and turn and be healed."* God decides who He loves unconditionally, and based on all the previous verses in this chapter, it isn't everyone.

Jesus knew His message of salvation would not be understood by Satan's followers. Jesus is the good shepherd and only His sheep listen to His voice and believe. <u>John 10: 26-27</u> *"but you do not believe because you are not my sheep. ²⁷ My sheep listen to my voice; I know them, and they follow me. ²⁸ I give them eternal life, and they shall never perish; no one will snatch them out of my hand."* God's sheep, His children, are blessed and understand His message of salvation.

Jesus talks about judgement day when He returns will separate His sheep on his right, believers, from non-believers, the goats on his left. <u>Matthews 25:34</u> *"Then the King will say to those on his right, 'Come, you who are blessed by my Father; take your inheritance, the kingdom prepared for you since the creation of the world."* Matthew 25:41 *"Then he will say to those on his left, 'Depart from me, you who are cursed, into the eternal fire prepared for the devil and his angels."* The cursed are the unbelievers who will spend eternity in Hell with Satan. Are the cursed loved by God unconditionally?

What is "Faith or Belief"?

Faith in God is not something that can be proven or seen. Faith is belief that one is saved by grace through faith in what Jesus Christ did for us on the cross. This is not a result of our works so that no one can boast of their good deeds before God or others. Again faith is all from God! Without God's Holy Spirit His Word would be foolishness to us. Hebrews 11:1 *"Now faith is being sure of what we hope for and certain of what we do not see."* How do we receive faith? Romans 10:17 *"Consequently, faith comes from hearing the message, and the message is heard through the word of Christ."* This means studying the Bible, attending church, joining a small bible study group etc.

I believe that if God wanted to save someone in a remote area in Africa, that He would find a method to reach that person with His Gospel message. Hearing God's message of salvation is essential in becoming a Christian. As stated earlier, a person must receive God's Holy Spirit in order to believe in Jesus as their Lord and savior. A person must also be continually filled with the Holy Spirit because we all leak.

I challenge anyone to find a promise of eternal life or salvation in the Bible without the condition of faith or belief. Psalm 101:3 *"I will not look with approval on anything that is vile. I hate what faithless people do; I will have no part in it"* If you can believe that God loves all those who will live in hell for eternity, with no chance of redemption, than I would concur that He loves everyone unconditionally. However, judging from God's treatment of people throughout the Old Testament, God loves those whom He saves by giving them His Holy Spirit, all others are lost and doomed to spend eternity in Hell. I am not ruling out the possibility that because of God's foreknowledge, that He knows who will reject Him, therefore He doesn't give them His Holy Spirit. Following are additional verses illustrating the requirement of faith/ belief and or obedience:

1. Matthew 7:21 *"Not everyone who says to me, 'Lord, Lord,' will enter the kingdom of heaven, but only the one who does the will of my Father who is in heaven.*" Isn't obedience a condition?

2. John 3:16 *"For God so loved the world that he gave his one and only Son, that whoever believes in him shall not perish but have eternal life."* Note the condition of "believing".

3. Mark 16:16 *"Whoever believes and is baptized will be saved, but whoever does not believe will be condemned."* Note that if you don't believe that you are condemned.

4. 1st John 5:5 *"Who is it that overcomes the world? Only he who believes that Jesus is the Son of God,"* Without belief or faith you will spend eternity in Hell.

5. Hebrews 11:6 *"And without faith it is impossible to please God, because anyone who comes to him must believe that he exists and that he rewards those who earnestly seek him.*

6. 1st John 5:10 *"Anyone who believes in the Son of God has this testimony in his heart. Anyone who does not believe God has made him out to be a liar, because he has not believed the testimony God has given about his Son."*

7. Romans 1:16-17 *"I am not ashamed of the gospel, because it is the power of God for the salvation of everyone who believes: first for the Jew, then for the Gentile. [17]For in the gospel a righteousness from God is revealed, a righteousness that is by faith from first to last, just as it is written: "The righteous will live by faith,"*

8. <u>Romans 2:13</u> *"For it is not those who hear the law who are righteous in God's sight, but it is those who obey the law who will be declared righteous".*

9. <u>Romans 3:22-26</u> *"This righteousness from God comes through faith in Jesus Christ to all who believe. There is no difference, [23]for all have sinned and fall short of the glory of God, [24]and are justified freely by his grace through the redemption that came by Christ Jesus. [25]God presented him as a sacrifice of atonement, through faith in his blood. He did this to demonstrate his justice, because in his forbearance he had left the sins committed beforehand unpunished— [26]he did it to demonstrate his justice at the present time, so as to be just and the one who justifies those who have faith in Jesus.*

Faith /belief is the major condition for man's salvation! Without Faith/belief you are lost and an antichrist destined for God's wrath!

God Had a Plan for Mankind

God is in control of His creation and has had a plan to repair the broken relationship caused by sin. Sin and death started way back in Garden of Eden and God promised to send a savior to repair that broken relationship. God inspired the Bible to be written so we could understand His expectations of us. It started with Moses where His chosen people were held in slavery in Egypt:

1. <u>Exodus 7:3</u> *"But I will harden Pharaoh's heart, and though I multiply my miraculous signs and wonders in Egypt, he will not listen to you."*

2. <u>Exodus 9:16</u> *"But I have raised you up for this very purpose, that I might show you my power and that my name might be proclaimed in all the earth."*

3. Exodus 10:1 *"Moses and Aaron performed all these wonders before Pharaoh, but the LORD hardened Pharaoh's heart, and he would not let the Israelites go out of his country."*

4. Exodus 11:10 *"Then the LORD said to Moses, "Go to Pharaoh, for I have hardened his heart and the hearts of his officials so that I may perform these signs of mine among them.*

5. "Exodus 12:36 *"The LORD had made the Egyptians favorably disposed toward the people, and they gave them what they asked for; so they plundered the Egyptians."* Sometimes God's methods are hard to understand.

6. Exodus 23:23 *"My angel will go ahead of you and bring you into the land of the Amorites, Hittites, Perizzites, Canaanites, Hivites and Jebusites, and I will wipe them out."*

7. Exodus 33:19 *"I will have mercy on whom I will have mercy, and I will have compassion on whom I will have compassion."*

8. Joshua 11:20 *"For it was the LORD himself who hardened their hearts to wage war against Israel, so that he might destroy them totally, exterminating them without mercy, as the LORD had commanded Moses."*

Ancient history showed little unconditional love toward God's enemies!

God Demands Obedience

What God desires or demands from His children is obedience. Even though God lets us chose our sins, He still wants us to keep His Commandments. King Saul learned the hard way about partial obedience. Because he failed to follow God's instructions completely, Saul lost God's Holy Spirit and later his Kingdom because of partial obedience. "Partial Obedience is Disobedience"!

Throughout the Bible God tells us to keep His commandments, to love Him and to fear Him:

1. Deuteronomy 6:24-25 *"The LORD commanded us to obey all these decrees and to fear the LORD our God, so that we might always prosper and be kept alive, as is the case today. ²⁵ And if we are careful to obey all this law before the LORD our God, as he has commanded us, that will be our righteousness."*

2. Deuteronomy 10:12-13 *"And now, O Israel, what does the LORD your God ask of you but to fear the LORD your God, to walk in all his ways, to love him, to serve the LORD your God with all your heart and with all your soul, ¹³ and to observe the LORD's commands and decrees that I am giving you today for your own good?"* Love and obedience were conditions of God's love.

3. Deuteronomy 11:1 *"Love the LORD your God and keep his requirements, his decrees, his laws and his commands always."* God prefers obedience over sacrifice!

4. 1st Samuel 15:22 *"But Samuel replied: "Does the LORD delight in burnt offerings and sacrifices as much as in obeying the voice of the LORD? To obey is better than sacrifice, and to heed is better than the fat of rams."*

Disobedience Has Consequences

God demands obedience and those who ignore God's laws pay a heavy price for their disobedience. However if they are a born again believer, they will repent and be forgiven.

1. Matthew 3:10 *"The ax is already at the root of the trees, and every tree that does not produce good fruit will be cut down and thrown into the fire."* True believers will produce good fruit. False Christians are those who are undistinguishable from unbelievers.

2. 1st Samuel 12-15 *"But if you do not obey the LORD, and if you rebel against his commands, his hand will be against you, as it was against your fathers."*

3. Deuteronomy 11:27-28 *" the blessing if you obey the commands of the LORD your God that I am giving you today;* 28 *the curse if you disobey the commands of the LORD your God and turn from the way that I command you today by following other gods, which you have not known."*

4. Leviticus 26:14-16 *"But if you will not listen to me and carry out all these commands,* 15 *and if you reject my decrees and abhor my laws and fail to carry out all my commands and so violate my covenant,* 16 *then I will do this to you: I will bring upon you sudden terror, wasting diseases and fever that will destroy your sight and drain away your life. You will plant seed in vain, because your enemies will eat it."*

5. Isaiah 1:19-20 *"If you are willing and obedient, you will eat the best from the land;* 20 *but if you resist and rebel, you will be devoured by the sword." For the mouth of the LORD has spoken."*

Conclusion

God does love His children, those He calls, elects, chooses or predestines! His love for His children is beyond comprehension:

1. Romans 8:1 *"Therefore, there is now no condemnation for those who are in Christ Jesus, [2] because through Christ Jesus the law of the Spirit who gives life has set you[a] free from the law of sin and death."*

2. Romans 8 28 *"And we know that in all things God works for the good of those who love him, who[i] have been called according to his purpose. [29] For those God foreknew he also predestined to be conformed to the image of his Son, that he might be the firstborn among many brothers and sisters.[30] And those he predestined, he also called; those he called, he also justified; those he justified, he also glorified. [31] What, then, shall we say in response to these things? If God is for us, who can be against us? [32] He who did not spare his own Son, but gave him up for us all—how will he not also, along with him, graciously give us all things? [33] Who will bring any charge against those whom God has chosen? It is God who justifies. [34] Who then is the one who condemns? No one. Christ Jesus who died—more than that, who was raised to life—is at the right hand of God and is also interceding for us. [35] Who shall separate us from the love of Christ? Shall trouble or hardship or persecution or famine or nakedness or danger or sword?"*

3. Romans 8:38 *"For I am convinced that neither death nor life, neither angels nor demons,[k] neither the present nor the future, nor any powers,[39] neither height nor depth, nor anything else in all creation, will be able to separate us from the love of God that is in Christ Jesus our Lord."*

Jesus was more critical of the "Religious Leaders" of his time than anyone else. Just because someone in authority gives you their opinion about unconditional love, that doesn't make it true. Paul said we should be like the Berean Christians and examine what scripture actually states.

No place in the Bible does it say that God loves anything

unconditionally, let alone everyone. Where then does this notion of unconditional love come from? I believe that it goes back to man's idol worship…man creating God in his own image rather than the true God in the Bible. Satan has been successful in getting many churches to proclaim that God loves everyone unconditionally for the politically correct.

Claiming God love everyone unconditionally is contrary to what the Bible actually teaches not to mention man's life experiences and world history. God's unconditional love for everyone either causes man to question the truth in God's Word or believe that sin has no consequences.

I am not questioning weather God loves His children, believers unconditionally. His love was evident by sending His Son, Jesus to die for us while we were still sinners. It is difficult for me to understand how someone could love a person unconditionally yet send them to a place where they would be tortured forever with no chance of repentance.

CHAPTER 6

THE TRUTH WILL SET YOU FREE

Myth # 4 Jesus is the "Prince of the World"

Who is the Real Prince of our World?

When people are asks, who the Bible says is the prince of the world, most will answer Jesus, even many Christians. Random House Dictionary defines Satan: *"the chief evil spirit: the great adversary of man: the devil."* The truth is that Satan is currently the "prince" of the world! The Bible also refers to him as the Devil. Jesus is the "Prince of Peace", He is the "Light of the World", the "Savor of the World" and "The Way, The Truth and The Light of the World". However, Satan or the Devil is the true "prince of the world" according to God's Word.

Satan is man's number one enemy as he seeks to destroy our relationship with God. Jesus referees to Satan as a thief that comes to destroy whereas Jesus comes to give man eternal life! John 10:10 *"The thief comes only to steal and kill and destroy; I have come that they may have life, and have it to the full".* Not just in this life but for eternity!

Satan is not someone to be ignored as he holds the power of death over the whole world.

1. Matthew 10:28 *"Do not be afraid of those who kill the body but cannot kill the soul. Rather, be afraid of the One who can destroy both soul and body in hell.*

2. 1 Peter 5:8 *"Be alert and of sober mind. Your enemy the devil prowls around like a roaring lion looking for someone to devour".*

3. John 4:15 *"Some people are like seed along the path, where the word is sown. As soon as they hear it, Satan comes and takes away the word that was sown in them."* Satan doesn't want God's Word to be remembered and acted upon._

4. Ephesians 6:12 *"For our struggle is not against flesh and blood, but against the rulers, against the authorities, against the powers of this dark world and against the spiritual forces of evil in the heavenly realms."* There is a Spiritual battle going on in the Heavenly Realms between Satan and God. Although God is more powerful than Satan, he is a force to be feared. Without God's help we are helpless against Satan's power.

5. 1 John 5:19 *"We know that we are children of God, and that the whole world is under the control of the evil one."* Satan's role is to lead the whole world astray! Without God's Spirit, man doesn't stand a chance against Satan's seductive ways.

6. John 16:11 *"and about judgment, because the prince of this world now stands condemned.* Satan and his followers will eventually spend eternity in Hell.

7. John 12:31 *"Now is the time for judgment on this world; now the prince of this world will be driven out."* Jesus is saying that Satan is currently the "prince of the world" but

someday he will be defeated and sent to Hell along with all his followers when Jesus returns.

How did Satan Come to Earth?

Satan was an angle created by God and can appear in many different forms:

1. In Genesis Satan appeared as a serpent. <u>Genesis 3:1</u> *"Now the serpent was more crafty than any of the wild animals the LORD God had made"*

2. Satan was thrown out of Heaven to earth because of his pride. Satan wanted to be God. <u>Revelations 12:9</u> *"The great dragon was hurled down—that ancient serpent called the devil, or Satan, who leads the whole world astray. He was hurled to the earth, and his angels with him."* Satan has many followers to help him lead the world astray. In the Garden of Eden, Satan was successful in getting Adam and Eve to believe his lie, that if they ate from "the tree of the knowledge of good and evil" that they wouldn't die. However, God clearly told them that if they ate of that tree they would surely die. Because of their disobedience all mankind has been under God's curse of death and decay.

3. <u>Luke 10:18</u> *He replied, "I saw Satan fall like lightning from heaven.* Satan and his minions were thrown out of Heaven to earth. Satan and his corrupt angles have led the whole world astray by getting man to worship self, possessions and power rather than God, the creator of everything.

Other Names for Satan

Satan and the Devil are interchangeable terms when talking about man's number one enemy. There are many other descriptive names for Satan, but because the whole world is under his control, "the prince of the world", best describes Satan. He is also known as "the serpent" and "the great dragon" as quoted previously.

1. <u>Prince of The World</u>: Jesus referred to Satan as "the prince of this world", who actually is an evil person in many different forms, not just an evil influence. <u>John 14:30</u> *"I will not say much more to you, for the prince of this world is coming. He has no hold over me,"* Only Jesus is able to resist Satan evil power.

2. <u>Accuser:</u> Satan is great at making us feel unworthy or guilty. <u>Zechariah 3:1</u> *"Then he showed me Joshua the high priest standing before the angel of the LORD, and Satan standing at his right side to accuse him."* However, Jesus died for all our sins, past, present and future. The only requirement to receive God's righteousness is believe in His Son. <u>Revelation 12:10</u> *"Now have come the salvation and the power and the kingdom of our God, and the authority of his Christ. For the accuser of our brothers, who accuses them before our God day and night, has been hurled down."* Satan knows our weaknesses and tries to take advantage of us when we are most vulnerable. However, Jesus won the battle over sin and death for all believers. Now Satan is condemned along with all unbelievers.

3. <u>Tempter:</u> Satan is also referred as "the tempter". <u>Matthew 4:3</u> *"The tempter came to him and said, "If you are the Son of God, tell these stones to become bread."* This happened after Jesus had not eaten for 40 days leaving Him extremely hungry. Jesus as God could easily could have created a feast out of the stones if He wanted to.

4. <u>Ruler of The Kingdom of the Air:</u> Another name given to Satan is "ruler of the kingdom of the air" <u>Ephesians 2:1 -2</u> *"As for you, you were dead in your transgressions and sins, in which you used to live when you followed the ways of this world and of the ruler of the kingdom of the air, the spirit who is now at work in those who are disobedient".* Only God is able to raise a dead spirit and make it alive in Him.

Antichrists are Actually Children of Satan

Antichrist is the newest term for Satin or one of his followers used in the New Testament.. The word "antichrist" means "against Christ". Antichrists are humans inhabited by Satan. Matthew was the first apostle to mention deceivers in his Gospel that falsely claimed to be "The Christ":

1. <u>Matthew 24:4-5</u> *"Jesus answered: "Watch out that no one deceives you. ⁵ For many will come in my name, claiming, 'I am the Messiah,' and will deceive many."* Later, the Apostle John called deceivers antichrists or one of Satan's followers:

2. <u>1 John 2:18</u> *"Dear children, this is the last hour; and as you have heard that the antichrist is coming, even now many antichrists have come. This is how we know it is the last hour.* The last hour began at Jesus' ascension into Heaven.

3. <u>1 John 2:22</u> *"Who is the liar? It is whoever denies that Jesus is the Christ. Such a person is the antichrist— denying the Father and the Son."* There millions of antichrists in the world as anyone who denies Jesus as their Lord and Savior is an antichrist.

4. <u>1 John 4:3</u>*" but every spirit that does not acknowledge Jesus*

is not from God. This is the spirit of the antichrist, which you have heard is coming and even now is already in the world".

5. 2 John 1:7 *"I say this because many deceivers, who do not acknowledge Jesus Christ as coming in the flesh, have gone out into the world. Any such person is the deceiver and the antichrist."* They will suffer the same fate as Satan. If you are not for Jesus then you are against Him! If not Jesus, then The Prince of this World" rules over your life!

Satan Must get Permission from God

In the book of Job, the Bible indicates that Satan had to get God's permission in order to act or do harm to man.

1. Job 1:6 *"One day the angels came to present themselves before the LORD, and Satan also came with them."* God challenged Satan to get Job to denounce Him.

2. Job 1:12 *"The LORD said to Satan, "Very well, then, everything he has is in your hands, but on the man himself do not lay a finger." Then Satan went out from the presence of the LORD."* God let Satan kill Job's children, destroy his livestock and destroy Job's home. Later, God gave Satan permission to cause physical harm but not to kill him.

3. Job 2:6-7 *"The LORD said to Satan, "Very well, then, he is in your hands; but you must spare his life."[7] So Satan went out from the presence of the LORD and afflicted Job with painful sores from the soles of his feet to the top of his head."*

In the end, God knew that Job would not fall away. Later Job was blessed way beyond all his previous possessions. Job obtained a powerful new faith and reverence for God, His creator.

Satan is the "prince of this world" for now, but only for as long as God/Jesus allows him to be in control. It is beyond man's intellect to understand why God allows Satan to continue his destruction on earth. Many times God has used Satan to accomplish his purpose by turning Satan's disaster into blessings. Man the created should not question God the creator.

Satan's Power vs God's Holy Spirit

God sent Jesus to defeat Satan and his power over death and decay. God desires to bring His children back into a relationship with Him. Only through Jesus is mankind able to conquer death resulting from man's sin! Only with God's Spirit is man able to overcome Satan's power.

1. Matthew 4:1 *"Then Jesus was led by the Spirit into the desert to be tempted by the devil."* This would not have happened if God did not permit it to happen.

2. Luke 4:1 *"Jesus, full of the Holy Spirit, left the Jordan and was led by the Spirit into the wilderness, ² where for forty days he was tempted by the devil. He ate nothing during those days, and at the end of them he was hungry."* Here God delivered Jesus to Satan, in order to show God's power over Satan.

3. Luke 22:31-32 *"Simon, Simon, Satan has asked to sift you as wheat. ³² But I have prayed for you, Simon, that your faith may not fail. And when you have turned back, strengthen your brothers."* Again, Satan had to ask Jesus' for permission to attack Peter.

How can We Resist Satan?

In order to resist Satan we must put on the full armor of God:

1. Ephesians 6:10-13 *"Finally, be strong in the Lord and in his mighty power. [11] Put on the full armor of God, so that you can take your stand against the devil's schemes. [12] For our struggle is not against flesh and blood, but against the rulers, against the authorities, against the powers of this dark world and against the spiritual forces of evil in the heavenly realms. [13] Therefore put on the full armor of God, so that when the day of evil comes, you may be able to stand your ground, and after you have done everything, to stand."* Paul was able to resist Elymas because he was full of the Holy Spirit. We must have the power of God's Spirit if we are to stand a chance against Satan!

2. 1st Peter 5:8 *"Be self-controlled and alert. Your enemy the devil prowls around like a roaring lion looking for someone to devour."*

3. Acts 13:9-10 *"Then Saul, who was also called Paul, filled with the Holy Spirit, looked straight at Elymas and said, [10]"You are a child of the devil and an enemy of everything that is right! You are full of all kinds of deceit and trickery. Will you never stop perverting the right ways of the Lord?"* Satan is not a cartoon character with horns and a pitchfork. He is an attractive, seductive, lethal enemy who knows all our weaknesses.

4. 2nd Corinthians 11:14 *"And no wonder, for Satan himself masquerades as an angel of light."* We are to flee from him and his temptations.

Unbelievers are Children of the Devil

The Bible states that unbelievers will not believe because they belonged to the devil. There is no middle ground; you are either a child of God or a child of the Satan.

1. Matthew 8:44 *"You belong to your father, the devil, and you want to carry out your father's desire. He was a murderer from the beginning, not holding to the truth, for there is no truth in him. When he lies, he speaks his native language, for he is a liar and the father of lies"*

2. 1st John 3:8-10 *"He who does what is sinful is of the devil, because the devil has been sinning from the beginning. The reason the Son of God appeared was to destroy the devil's work. ⁹No one who is born of God will continue to sin, because God's seed remains in him; he cannot go on sinning, because he has been born of God. ¹⁰This is how we know who the children of God are and who the children of the devil are: Anyone who does not do what is right is not a child of God; nor is anyone who does not love his brother."*

3. John 6:70 *"Then Jesus replied, "Have I not chosen you, the Twelve? Yet one of you is a devil!"* Jesus was talking about Judas His betrayer as a devil. God was in control of Judas as he was part of God's plan to bring man back into a relationship with Him. God's plan after man's fall goes way back to Genesis. Genesis 3:15 *"And I will put enmity between you and the woman, and between your offspring and hers; he will crush your head, and you will strike his heel."* Man will eventually crush Satan's head only with God's help. In the meantime, Satan will strike mankind until God decides it is time for Satan and all his followers to be thrown into the lake of fire.

God Uses Satan to Accomplish His Purpose

God used God uses Satan to accomplish His purpose:

1. 1st Samuel 16:14-15 *"Now the Spirit of the LORD had departed from Saul, and an evil spirit from the LORD*

tormented him. [15] *Saul's attendants said to him, "See, an evil spirit from God is tormenting you.* Eventually God had Saul killed and David took over as King of the Jews.

2. 1st Corinthian 5:5 "*hand this man over to Satan, so that the sinful nature may be destroyed and his spirit saved on the day of the Lord."*

3. 1st Timothy 1:20 *"Among them are Hymenaeus and Alexander, whom I have handed over to Satan to be taught not to blaspheme."* God turned these men over to Satanto be punished by Satan.

4. 2nd Corinthians 12:7 *"To keep me from becoming conceited because of these surpassingly great revelations, there was given me a thorn in my flesh, a messenger of Satan, to torment me."* God told Paul that His grace was sufficient and refused to heal him. God wants us to depend on Him and not take Him and all His gifts for granted.

God's plans for Satan

It is impossible in most instances for man to distinguish between the Children of God from the Children of the Satan. Only God knows man's heart. In the following verse, the weeds and the wheat were impossible for the farmer to distinguish one from another. Matthew 13:25 *"But while everyone was sleeping, his enemy came and sowed weeds among the wheat, and went away."* In this parable, the weeds represented the children of the Devil/Satan and the wheat represented the children of God. Since the farmer couldn't tell the difference, he had to wait until maturity when there was a distinct difference. Jesus goes on to explain what happens to them at the end of the age. Matthew 13:38-39 "*The field is the world, and the good seed stands for the sons of the kingdom. The weeds are the sons of the evil one,* [39] *and the enemy who sows them is the devil. The harvest is the end of the age, and the harvesters are angels."*

We don't know who Satan's children are nor are we to judge our neighbor. However, God knows who will accept Him and who will reject Him and His Son. Some people don't come to accept Jesus as their Lord and Savor until they are very old while others may come to him at an early age. The thief on the cross believed in Jesus just before he died and went to paradise with Jesus. Luke 23:43 *"Jesus answered him, "Truly I tell you, today you will be with me in paradise."*

A key reason why many people don't understand God's word is that they are under the control of the Satan and considered an antichrist. Revelations 19:9-20 *"We know that we are children of God, and that the whole world is under the control of the evil one. [20]We know also that the Son of God has come and has given us understanding, so that we may know him who is true. And we are in him who is true—even in his Son Jesus Christ. He is the true God and eternal life."* Believers have God's Holy Spirit which has opened up their minds to understand God's truth.

Satan, along with all unbelievers, antichrists, has a future already been determined by God since the beginning:

1. Revelations 20:15 *"Anyone whose name was not found written in the book of life was thrown into the lake of fire".*

2. Revelations 19:20 *" But the beast was captured, and with it the false prophet who had performed the signs on its behalf. With these signs he had deluded those who had received the mark of the beast and worshiped its image. The two of them were thrown alive into the fiery lake of burning sulfur".*

3. Revelation 20:10 *"And the devil, who deceived them, was thrown into the lake of burning sulfur, where the beast and the false prophet had been thrown. They will be tormented day and night for ever and ever."* Antichrist's will receive the same punishment as Satan.

4. Revelations 21:8 *"But the cowardly, the unbelieving, the vile, the murderers, the sexually immoral, those who*

practice magic arts, the idolaters and all liars —they will be consigned to the fiery lake of burning sulfur. This is the second death."

Man must be born again and accept Jesus's His forgiveness for all their sins or suffer God's 'eternal wrath as an antichrist. Although Satan is "the prince of this world" for now, his days are numbered. Someday, Jesus will take His rightful place as "King of Kings" and "Lord of Lords" when God determines the time is right!

CHAPTER 7

THE TRUTH WILL SET YOU FREE

Myth # 5: Jesus is "A" Way to Heaven

Political Correctness is all "Gray"

Political correctness has reached a ridiculous level in our society. The truth has been diluted as to not offend anyone. Political correctness only speaks in terms of gray. In God's mind there is no gray, everything is either true or it is false, black or white! You are either for Jesus or you are His enemy! Matthew 12:30 *"He who is not with me is against me, and he who does not gather with me scatters"* The truth about life is that you are either a believer, a child of God, or an antichrist, a child of Satan.

Jesus Is the "Only Way" to Heaven

Do Moslems, Buddhists, Hindus, Jews etc. all have a different path leading to the same eternal life Heaven, as Christians? If Moslems firmly believe in the teachings of Mohammed and follow his teachings, do they also go to Heaven? Many people of different faiths believe Jesus is "**a**" means by which Christians get to Heaven but there are also other ways/means for peoples of different faiths. However, that is not what God's Word clearly says:

1. <u>Acts 4:12</u> *"Salvation is found in no one else, for there is no other name under heaven given to men by which we must be saved."*

2. <u>John 14:6</u> *"Jesus answered, "I am the way and the truth and the life. No one comes to the Father except through me."*

3. <u>Matthew 1:21:</u> *"She will give birth to a son, and you are to give him the name Jesus, because he will save his people from their sins."* "His people" are God's chosen, elect, redeemed, called or predestined for salvation, the saved. All others are lost.

4. <u>John 1:14)</u> *"The Word became flesh and made his dwelling among us. We have seen his glory, the glory of the one and only Son, who came from the Father, full of grace and truth"* The Word, was God, He became flesh, Jesus, full of grace and truth.

5. <u>Acts 10:43</u> *"All the prophets testify about him that everyone who believes in him receives forgiveness of sins through his name."*

6. <u>1 Timothy 2:5</u> *" For there is one God and one mediator between God and mankind, the man Christ Jesus,"* Jesus was and is our mediator before Holy God.

Jesus clearly stated that He is **THE** only way, not **A** way to God the Father. This sounds exclusive but <u>John 3:16</u> states that Jesus died for whole world's sins which couldn't be more inclusive. The only requirement is faith/ belief in the truth about Jesus in the Bible.

Why would God put His only Son through the most painful, the most humiliating death imaginable if there was another way of salvation?

Remember, no one can earn their way into Heaven! Since we all sin, there is only one way to receive forgiveness and that is through belief in what Jesus did for us on the cross. He paid the penalty for all our sins past, present and future!

No other religion can offer the forgiveness of sins. All other religions require works in order to please God. No amount of "good works" will ever be enough to earn a place in Heaven. Psalms 49:7-9 *"No man can redeem the life of another or give to God a ransom for him-* [8] *the ransom for a life is costly, no payment is ever enough-* [9] *that he should live on forever and not see decay."*

Christianity is 100% God!

The empty tomb of Jesus proves that He is God's one and only son. Mohammed and Buddha are buried in a tomb that people can visit. The Romans authorities and Jewish religious leaders left no stone unturned in trying to find Jesus' body and disprove Jesus' resurrection. They couldn't find Jesus body because God resurrected Jesus to be at His right hand. Hundreds of witnesses saw Jesus after his crucifixion and Jesus' disciples witnessed His assertion:

1. Acts 1:*3* *"After his suffering, he showed himself to these men and gave many convincing proofs that he was alive. He appeared to them over a period of forty days and spoke about the kingdom of God."*

2. Acts 1:9-11 *"After he said this, he was taken up before their very eyes, and a cloud hid him from their sight.* [10]*They were looking intently up into the sky as he was going, when suddenly two men dressed in white stood beside them.* [11]*"Men of Galilee," they said, "why do you stand here looking into the sky? This same Jesus, who has been taken from you into heaven, will come back in the same way you have seen him go into heaven."*

3. Luke 24:50-**51** *"When he had led them out to the vicinity of Bethany, he lifted up his hands and blessed them. [51]While he was blessing them, he left them and was taken up into heaven."*

4. Acts 10:40-41 *"but God raised him from the dead on the third day and caused him to be seen. [41]He was not seen by all the people, but by witnesses whom God had already chosen—by us who ate and drank with him after he rose from the dead."*

The greatest proof that Jesus was who he claimed to be is the fact that all His disciples were martyred except John who died in exiled. No one would die for something they didn't believe in!

Those Who Deny Jesus are Condemned

There are only two ways someone is able to entering into Heaven: Living a perfect sinless life on earth or the belief in that Jesus paid the full price for all my sins.

Since the Bible clearly states that no one can live a sinless life, only the belief in Jesus' sacrifice on the cross is the only other option for eternal life in Heaven:

1. John 3:36 *"Whoever believes in the Son has eternal life, but whoever rejects the Son will not see life, for God's wrath remains on him."*

2. John 3:18 *"Whoever believes in him is not condemned, but whoever does not believe stands condemned already because he has not believed in the name of God's one and only Son."*

3. Romans 8:1 *"Therefore, there is now no condemnation for those who are in Christ Jesus"* All nonbelievers are commended to eternal damnation.

As stated earlier, without the Holy Spirit, God's Word is foolishness. Unbelievers will continue on the "broad road" that leads to destruction:

1. <u>1 Corinthians 1:18</u> *"For the message of the cross is foolishness to those who are perishing, but to us who are being saved it is the power of God".*

2. <u>1 Corinthians 2:14</u> *"The man without the Spirit does not accept the things that come from the Spirit of God, for they are foolishness to him, and he cannot understand them, because they are spiritually discerned."*

What About God's Chosen People?

Throughout the Old Testament blood sacrifices were offered for the forgiveness of the Jewish people's sins. The high priest would sacrifice lambs, bulls and other animals as a sin offering. The man's sins were transferred to an unblemished lamb that was then slaughtered. The lamb's shed blood paid the price of the man's sins. This had to be repeated over and over again as everyone continually sins. This Old Testament method for the forgiveness of man's sins was forever changed when Jesus, true Lamb of God shed His blood on the Cross once for all:

1. <u>Leviticus 17:11</u> *"For the life of a creature is in the blood, and I have given it to you to make atonement for yourselves on the altar; it is the blood that makes atonement for one's life."* Without the shedding of blood there is no forgiveness.

2. <u>Hebrews 9:22</u> *"In fact, the law requires that nearly everything be cleansed with blood, and without the shedding of blood there is no forgiveness."* This was all a precursor to total forgiveness through Jesus' shed blood on the cross. Jesus, "the Lamb of God" shed His bloods once and for all who believe in Him.

Ever since the destruction of the Jewish temple in 70AD, no sacrifices for the forgiveness of sins have been offered. How are the Jewish People's sins forgiven without blood sacrifices? Jesus' shed His blood on the cross for all believers' sins. However if you deny Jesus then you will die in your sins! It is not for anyone to judge what happens to God's chosen people, the Jews, or anyone else when they die:

1. Romans 11:11 *"Again I ask: Did they stumble so as to fall beyond recovery? Not at all! Rather, because of their transgression, salvation has come to the Gentiles to make Israel envious."* The Jews will eventually be grafted back into God's group of believers:

2. Romans 11:25-27 *"I do not want you to be ignorant of this mystery, brothers and sisters, so that you may not be conceited: Israel has experienced a hardening in part until the full number of the Gentiles has come in,* [26] *and in this way all Israel will be saved. As it is written: "The deliverer will come from Zion; he will turn godlessness away from Jacob. And this is my covenant with them when I take away their sins."*

3. Romans 11:19-21 *"You will say then, "Branches were broken off so that I could be grafted in."* [20] *Granted. But they were broken off because of unbelief, and you stand by faith. Do not be arrogant, but tremble.* [21] *For if God did not spare the natural branches, he will not spare you either."* Gentiles are not to become prideful of their salvation as God will not tolerate their unbelief either.

What About Billions of Moslems?

Questions to consider about Muslim countries:

1. Why is almost every Moslem country controlled by a dictator?

2. Why are most of their people uneducated and live in poverty?

3. Why is freedom of religion not tolerated?

4. Why is punishment for unbelief in Allah so severe? Convert to Islam, pay tribute forever or be killed.

Unfortunately they are like sheep being led to the slaughter. Only God knows who among them will come to the true God of the Bible.

Although there have been many crimes committed in the name of God, the New Covenant under Christ teaches love and forgiveness. Jesus came into the world to save sinners not to condemn them. John 3:17 *"For God did not send his Son into the world to condemn the world, but to save the world through him.* All other religions or beliefs will only lead to God's condemnation. Believers in false religions, those who deny Jesus as God's Only Son who suffered and died for their sins, will die in their sins!

Jesus also taught us not to seek revenge but to turn the other cheek when struck. Matthew 5:38-42 *"You have heard that it was said, 'Eye for eye, and tooth for tooth.'* [39] *But I tell you, do not resist an evil person. If anyone slaps you on the right cheek, turn to them the other cheek also.* [40] *And if anyone wants to sue you and take your shirt, hand over your coat as well.* [41] *If anyone forces you to go one mile, go with them two miles.* [42] *Give to the one who asks you, and do not turn away from the one who wants to borrow from you."* Jesus even forgave those who tortured and were about to kill Him. Luke 23:34 *"Jesus said, "Father, forgive them, for they do not know what they are doing."* ___

How do I know if I Am "Born Again"?

One must be born again of water and the spirit in order to see the kingdom of God:

1. John 3:3 *"In reply Jesus declared, "I tell you the truth, no one can see the kingdom of God unless he is born again."*

2. John 3:5 *"Jesus answered, "I tell you the truth, no one can enter the kingdom of God unless he is born of water and the Spirit."* When you are born again you are a "new" person. If there is no change in your behavior, then you are not born of the spirit!

Someone "born again" has received the gift of God's Holy Spirit. Those who are born again enter through the "narrow gate" that leads to life. The wicked will not enter the kingdom of heaven. 1 Corinthians 6:9 *"Do you not know that the wicked will not inherit the kingdom of God? Do not be deceived: Neither the sexually immoral nor idolaters nor adulterers nor male prostitutes nor homosexual offenders [10] nor thieves nor the greedy nor drunkards nor slanderers nor swindlers will inherit the kingdom of God."* There is still hope of rebirth up until someone takes their last breath. The thief on the cross received the gift of eternal life with Christ hours before he died.

Additional Bible passages that clearly state that the only one way into Heaven is through belief in Jesus' sacrifice, death and resurrection.

1. Matthew 10:32-33 *"Whoever acknowledges me before men, I will also acknowledge him before my Father in heaven. [33] But whoever disowns me before men, I will disown him before my Father in heaven.*

2. 1 John 5:4-5 *"for everyone born of God overcomes the world. This is the victory that has overcome the world, even our faith. [5] Who is it that overcomes the world? Only he who believes that Jesus is the Son of God."*

3. John 5:10 *"Anyone who believes in the Son of God has this testimony in his heart. Anyone who does not believe God has made him out to be a liar, because he has not believed the testimony God has given about his Son."*

4. John 8:24 *"I told you that you would die in your sins; if you do not believe that I am the one I claim to be, you will indeed die in your sins."*

5. John 8:47 *"He who belongs to God hears what God says. The reason you do not hear is that you do not belong to God."*

God Desires Obedience Not Sacrifice

God is not impressed with gifts or works as much as He is impressed with obedience and following his commandments:

1. Mark 12:33 *"To love him with all your heart, with all your understanding and with all your strength, and to love your neighbor as yourself is more important than all burnt offerings and sacrifices."* We are to walk the talk not just have knowledge of God's Commandments. Over and over again the Bible states God's desire of obedience which leads to righteousness which leads to Heaven. Sin makes us a slave whereas obedience makes sets us free.

2. Romans 6:16 *"Don't you know that when you offer yourselves to someone to obey him as slaves, you are slaves to the one whom you obey—whether you are slaves to sin, which leads to death, or to obedience, which leads to righteousness?"*

3. Matthew 19:17 *"Why do you ask me about what is good?" Jesus replied. "There is only One who is good. If you want to enter life, obey the commandments."*

4. John 14:23-24 *"Jesus replied, "If anyone loves me, he will obey my teaching. My Father will love him, and we will come to him and make our home with him.* [24]*He who does not love me will not obey my teaching. These words you hear are not my own; they belong to the Father who sent me."*

5. Hebrews 5:9 *"and, once made perfect, he became the source of eternal salvation for all who obey him"* Obedience is not optional it is essential for eternal life!

Jesus Confirms the Old Testament

Many believe that the New Testament is the "New Covenant" with God. They believe the Old Testament doesn't apply to Christians any more? The truth is that Jesus wouldn't change anything written in the Old Testament. Matthews 5:17-18 *"Do not think that I have come to abolish the Law or the Prophets; I have not come to abolish them but to fulfill them. ¹⁸I tell you the truth, until heaven and earth disappear, not the smallest letter, not the least stroke of a pen, will by any means disappear from the Law until everything is accomplished.* The Old Testament forecasts and promises a savior, the coming of a Messiah and the New Testament is the fulfillment of those promises.

Conclusion:

Without God's unconditional love for His Children, no one would be spared God's wrath or eternal damnation. Because God is a just God and hates sin, He provided a way out for His children or believers in Him and His word. Jesus suffered and died in order to pay the penalty for all the sins of believers. Jesus' resurrection proved that He was God and His follower's would someday also rise from the dead. Romans 5:19 *"For just as through the disobedience of the one man the many were made sinners, so also through the obedience of the one man the many will be made righteous".*

No other religion offers forgiveness and no one is good enough to earn their way into Heaven. Christianity is God's effort in order to reunite sinful man into fellowship with Him after the great fall of Adam and Eve.

CHAPTER 8

THE TRUTH WILL SET YOU FREE

Myth # 6: "Natural Man" is "Basically Good"

Man is Sinful at Birth!

Many people believe that man is born sinless but learns about sin from their environment. The truth is sin is in all our genes at birth. <u>Psalm 51:5</u> *"Surely I was sinful at birth, sinful from the time my mother conceived me."* If man doesn't acknowledge his sin, he won't look for a solution to sin and rationalize his/her destructive nature. Sin separates us from God and it is only through God's mercy and grace that anyone is spared God's wrath. <u>Romans 6:23</u> *"For the wages of sin is death, but the gift of God is eternal life in Christ Jesus our Lord."*

We all sin and fall short of God's standard of perfection:

1. <u>Psalm 58:3</u> *"Even from birth the wicked go astray; from the womb they are wayward and speak lies."*

2. <u>Psalm 143:2</u> *"Do not bring your servant into judgment, for no one living is righteous before you.*

3. <u>Ecclesiastes 7:20</u> *"There is not a righteous man on earth who does what is right and never sins."*

4. <u>1st John 1:8</u> *"If we claim to be without sin, we deceive ourselves and the truth is not in us.*

5. <u>1st John 1:10</u> *"If we claim we have not sinned, we make him out to be a liar and his word has no place in our lives.*

Most people try to rationalize their sins by comparing their sins with others that they believe to be a greater sinner. We are quick to judge our neighbor's sins but often unaware of our own sins. <u>Matthew 7:3-5</u> *"Why do you look at the speck of sawdust in your brother's eye and pay no attention to the plank in your own eye?* [4]*How can you say to your brother, 'Let me take the speck out of your eye,' when all the time there is a plank in your own eye?* [5]*You hypocrite, first take the plank out of your own eye, and then you will see clearly to remove the speck from your brother's eye."*

Sin is Mans Greatest Problem

Until we acknowledge we have a serious sin problem, we will not seek a solution. Just as the drug addict or alcoholic will never conquer his/her addiction until they admit that they are addicted. Without God's Holy Spirit, man will continue to rationalizing their sins. Only through the power of the Holy Spirit, are we able to see our sinful behavior and repent, which is turning around away from our sin and back toward God.

Jesus' death and sacrifice on the cross paid the price "in full" for all man's sins. However we must believe in Jesus and accept his free gift of salvation. If we deny Jesus He will deny us and we will be condemned and die in our sins.

Sin Began with Satan Wanting to be God

Satan was Gods Head Angle and fell from God's grace when he demanded to be like God. Adam and Eve followed suite when tempted by Satan in the Garden of Eden. Satan convinced them that if they disobeyed God that they would be like God. <u>Genesis 3:4-5</u> *"You will not surely die," the serpent said to the woman. ⁵"For God knows that when you eat of it your eyes will be opened, and you will be like God, knowing good and evil."* Death has been man's punishment ever sense. Success brings out our pride which leads to a feeling of self reliance and alienation from God. <u>Proverbs 30:7-9</u> *"Two things I ask of you, O LORD; do not refuse me before I die:* ⁸ *Keep falsehood and lies far from me; give me neither poverty nor riches, but give me only my daily bread.* ⁹ *Otherwise, I may have too much and disown you and say, 'Who is the LORD ' Or I may become poor and steal, and so dishonor the name of my God."* What a great prayer!

God created man to be in perfect union with Him and all this went well until "sin" came into the world. sin is what separates us from God! Note that: *"There is no" I" in team but "I" is right in the middle of sin."*

Satan is more powerful than any individual. Ever since Adams and Eve's sin, God provided a way out of our sin condition which lead to death ever since. God promised a Savior throughout the Old Testament and finally fulfilled His promise in the New Testament through Jesus the promised Messiah. God offered His only Son to pay the price for the sins of the world through Jesus' sacrifice, His shed blood, on the cross. All believers who believe Jesus died for their sins and rose from the dead are God's children and seen as righteous in His eyes. Unfortunately all unbelievers are condemned and considered children of Satan who will die in their sins and spend eternity in Hell.

No one Deserves Salvation

Many unbelievers think that God weighs the good you have done vs. the evil. As long as the good outweighs the bad, you will spend eternity in Heaven. The problem with that theory is that God demands perfection. <u>Matthew 5:48</u> *"Be perfect, therefore, as your heavenly Father is perfect."* Denying that there is a God makes unbelievers to be a fool. <u>Psalm 14:1-3 & 53:1-3</u> *"The fool says in his heart, "There is no God." They are corrupt, and their ways are vile; there is no one who does good. ²The LORD looks down from heaven on the sons of men to see if there are any who understand, any who seek God. ³All have turned aside, they have together become corrupt; there is no one who does good, not even one."*

Left on our own, we will never seek God. <u>Romans 3:10-18</u> *"As it is written: "There is no one righteous, not even one; ¹¹there is no one who understands, no one who seeks God. ¹²All have turned away, they have together become worthless; there is no one who does good, not even one." ¹³"Their throats are open graves; their tongues practice deceit. "The poison of vipers is on their lips¹⁴"Their mouths are full of cursing and bitterness. ¹⁵"Their feet are swift to shed blood; ¹⁶ruin and misery mark their ways, ¹⁷and the way of peace they do not know." ¹⁸"There is no fear of God before their eyes."*

We all are sinners deserving death, and without God's Holy Spirit, no one will even seek God. Left on our own we don't stand a chance of resisting Satan and the seduction of the world. *"Sin is man's poison and Jesus is the only antidote!"*

We are all Racists and Hypocrites

Everyone discriminates to some extent either in regard to race, social/economic conditions gender, education, looks, dress or where someone lives. Racism in God's eyes is thinking or acting as if we are superior to someone else in any of the above examples. Racism is concealed pride which is something which God hates! Most jokes and gossip are made up of one or more forms of racism. We all are guilty of racism to some degree.

Jesus gave us a perfect example to follow when He met the Samaritan woman at the well:

1. First, she was a Samaritan which was considered to be inferior to the Jews.

2. Second, she was a woman and in that culture women were considered to be inferior to men plus she was alone which also was inappropriate behavior for a woman to be unaccompanied by either other women or by male family members.

3. Third, Jesus knew she was living an immoral life. However Jesus came and talked to her which changed her whole life around.

Hypocrisy is another universal fault in man. We are able to see the fault in our spouse or someone else but fail to see our own faults or sins. Jesus told us to first remove the plank in our own eye before we try to remove the speck of sawdust in our brother's eye. Luke 6:41-42 *"Why do you look at the speck of sawdust in your brother's eye and pay no attention to the plank in your own eye?* [42] *How can you say to your brother, 'Brother, let me take the speck out of your eye,' when you yourself fail to see the plank in your own eye? You hypocrite, first take the plank out of your eye, and then you will see clearly to remove the speck from your brother's eye."* A great comeback when someone claims that they don't go to church because there so many hypocrites there, tell them: *"yes, but there is always room for one more hypocrite."*

What is sin?

Sin is not living up to God's standard of perfection, it is "missing the mark" or falling short of God's Commandments. God demands us to be perfect. Sin causes man to worship self rather than God. James, the brother of Jesus claims that if we break one of God's laws we are guilty of breaking all of His commandments. James 2:10 *"For whoever keeps the whole law and yet stumbles at just one point is guilty of breaking all of it."* Only Jesus was able to live a perfect, sinless life. Everyone else sins and is deserving of death! <u>Romans 6:23</u> *"For the wages of sin is death, but the gift of God is eternal life in Christ Jesus our Lord."* The closer we come to God, the greater our awareness of our sins.

I saw a clever sign in front of a church that read: *"The wages of sin is death. Repent before payday!"* The reason man should fear God is that only He can forgive all of our sins. Because God is also a just God, therefore sin must be accounted for.

God's Word clearly states that blood must be shed in order for sins to be forgiven. <u>Hebrews 9:22</u> *"In fact, the law requires that nearly everything be cleansed with blood, and without the shedding of blood there is no forgiveness."* In the Old Testament the priests sacrificed animals for the atonement of the people's sin on a regular basis. Today Christ's shed blood has paid the price for all man's sin so there is no need of further animal blood sacrifices. The only condition of man's forgiveness is that we accept Jesus' sacrifice on the cross as payment for our sins, that He died and rose from the dead and is in Heaven at the right hand of the God the Father.

God's Commandments Are for Man's Benefit

The 10 Commandments were not written to take away our fun in life, but for our protection. If everyone on earth kept all God's commandments, we would come close to heaven here on earth. Imagine a world without the need of an army or a police force, where everyone thought more of others than their selves.

Pride is the Devil's most successful weapon used to separate us from God. Pride causes us to take credit for God's blessings and causes us to covet what others have. Remember, God is a jealous God and a powerful God. All blessings come from God and only God is able to forgive our sins. <u>Proverbs 16:18</u> *"Pride goes before destruction, a haughty spirit before a fall."*

Over the past 100 years, churches have been downplaying the effect of sin on man's relationship with God and our neighbors. Believing there is a God is important but even the demons believes that there is a God. James 2:19 *"You believe that there is one God. Good! Even the demons believe that—and shudder."*

Living a righteous life is only possible through the help of God's Holy Spirit. Faith without action is not true faith. James 2:17 *"In the same way, faith by itself, if it is not accompanied by action, is dead."* James 2:20 *"You foolish man, do you want evidence that faith without deeds is useless?"*

Man's duty is to follow God's commandments. Ecclesiastes 12:13 *"Now all has been heard; here is the conclusion of the matter: Fear God and keep his commandments, for this is the whole duty of man"* Note that they are "commandments" not "suggestions"!

The 10 Commandments contains behavior that the majority of people around the world agree with. What do atheist and organizations like the ACLU have against publishing The 10 Commandments in public? Are they against honoring their parents? Are they in favor of murder? Are they in favor of adultery, stealing and lying? I guess those who oppose The 10 Commandments also think it is okay to covet others possessions.

The following commandments are engraved in the USA, the Supreme Court. They also were accepted for over 200 years in all public intuitions through out the country. Today the antichrists are doing everything in their power to remove anything to do with God.

The 10 Commandments:

<u>1st **Commandment**</u> <u>Exodus 20:3</u> *"You shall have no other gods before me.* God is to be #1 in your life! Either the God of the Bible is the only true God or He is a fraud. If we worship any other God we are worshiping a lie and will bear God's wrath. Worshiping the God of chance, evolution, is very high risk. The consequences of being wrong are severe and eternal!

<u>2nd **Commandment**</u> <u>Exodus 20:4-6</u> *"You shall not make for yourself an idol in the form of anything in heaven above or on the earth*

beneath or in the waters below. [5] *You shall not bow down to them or worship them; for I, the LORD your God, am a jealous God, punishing the children for the sin of the fathers to the third and fourth generation of those who hate me,* [6] *but showing love to a thousand {generations} of those who love me and keep my commandments.* Do not worship Idols! Idols don't have to be in the form statues of other god's, they can be anything that you value more than God. Idols can be your children, your spouse, your possessions, power etc. Anything that comes before God in your life is an idol.

3rd Commandment Exodus 20:7 *"You shall not misuse the name of the LORD your God, for the LORD will not hold anyone guiltless who misuses his name.* Do not use God's name irreverently. The Bible says that we will be accountable for every careless word spoken. Using God's name in vane is one of the greatest insults to the God of the Universe and shows no respect for Him. Matthew 12:36-37 *"But I tell you that men will have to give account on the day of judgment for every careless word they have spoken.* [37]*For by your words you will be acquitted, and by your words you will be condemned."*

4th Commandment Exodus 20:8-11 *"Remember the Sabbath day by keeping it holy.* [9] *Six days you shall labor and do all your work,* [10] *but the seventh day is a Sabbath to the LORD your God. On it you shall not do any work, neither you, nor your son or daughter, nor your manservant or maidservant, nor your animals, nor the alien within your gates.* [11] *For in six days the LORD made the heavens and the earth, the sea, and all that is in them, but he rested on the seventh day. Therefore the LORD blessed the Sabbath day and made it holy.* Man should keep one day a week for rest and worship. Resting on the Sabbath is not just for honoring God, but for our own good. We need rest from our busy lives and God wants us to use the Sabbath for quality family time together. When I was growing up retail stores were closed on Sunday which was a day families would have a meal together and an opportunity to spend quality time together.

5th Commandment Exodus 20:12 *"Honor your father and your mother, so that you may live long in the land the LORD your God is giving you.* Respect your parents! Parents should be good role models for their children and honor their parents. If children don't respect their parents or attend church or study God's Word, what chance do their children have of becoming a believer? It has been said that Christianity is just one generation away from extinction. It is amazing how smart parents become after we become adults.

6th Commandment Exodus 20:13 *"You shall not murder.* Commandments 6-9 are universal in almost every culture. Many people have changed the true meaning from murder to "kill". God commanded His chosen people to kill on many occasions and commanded capital punishment for severe crimes against the local government.

7th Commandment Exodus 20:14 *"You shall not commit adultery.* God invented sex for increasing the population of the earth and for human enjoyment. Sex with a married person other than our spouse destroys families. Children are the greatest victims of an adulteress affair. Children suffer when raised in single parent home and are more likely to turn to drugs and crime.

8th Commandment Exodus 20:15 *"You shall not steal.* Every civilized culture has laws against stealing. Are you stealing from God by not giving back any of your time and your money?

9th Commandment Exodus 20:16 *"You shall not give false testimony against your neighbor.* We are not to lie! Truth is what our legal system is built on. Truth builds trust and builds strong relationships. In God's eyes "white lies" are lies!

10th Commandment Exodus 20:17 *"You shall not covet your neighbor's house. You shall not covet your neighbor's wife, or his manservant or maidservant, his ox or donkey, or anything that belongs to your neighbor."* Do not be envious of others possessions!

Coveting is not being happy with what we have been given by God. The Bible says that we should be content in all situations. 1st Thessalonians 5:16-17 *"Be joyful always; ¹⁷pray continually; ¹⁸give thanks in all circumstances, for this is God's will for you in Christ Jesus."*

God's Solution to Sin and Satan

Sin is not of God but of the Devil.1st John 3:8 *"He who does what is sinful is of the devil, because the devil has been sinning from the beginning. The reason the Son of God appeared was to destroy the devil's work."* God understands that man has no control over their sinful nature. Paul talks about this in Romans 7:18-20 *"I know that nothing good lives in me, that is, in my sinful nature, For I have the desire to do what is good, but I cannot carry it out. ¹⁹For what I do is not the good I want to do; no, the evil I do not want to do—this I keep on doing. ²⁰Now if I do what I do not want to do, it is no longer I who do it, but it is sin living in me that does it."* Natural man is a slave to sin!

The good news is that God has a solution for His chosen to their sin problem. Romans 8:1-2 *"Therefore, there is now no condemnation for those who are in Christ Jesus, ²because through Christ Jesus the law of the Spirit of life set me free from the law of sin and death."* Because of our sin all deserve death or eternal punishment in Hell. However, because of God's mercy and grace He chooses to save some, His children, even though all are ungodly and deserve death. Romans 5:6-8 *"You see, at just the right time, when we were still powerless, Christ died for the ungodly. ⁷Very rarely will anyone die for a righteous man, though for a good man someone might possibly dare to die. ⁸But God demonstrates his own love for us in this: While we were still sinners, Christ died for us."* Again, God's solution for our "sin problem" is all God!

God withholds His Holy Spirit to the children of Satan and give them over to their sinful nature. Psalm 81:12 *"So I gave them over to their stubborn hearts to follow their own devices."* Romans 1:24-25

"Therefore God gave them over in the sinful desires of their hearts to sexual impurity for the degrading of their bodies with one another. [25]They exchanged the truth of God for a lie, and worshiped and served created things rather than the Creator"

Man's Solution to Sin:

God knows that we all sin and will forgive us if we confess our sins and repent:

1. 1st John 1:8-10 *"If we claim to be without sin, we deceive ourselves and the truth is not in us. [9]If we confess our sins, he is faithful and just and will forgive us our sins and purify us from all unrighteousness. [10]If we claim we have not sinned, we make him out to be a liar and his word has no place in our lives.*

2. 1st Corinthians 6:18 *"Flee from sexual immorality. All other sins a man commits are outside his body, but he who sins sexually sins against his own body. [19]Do you not know that your body is a temple of the Holy Spirit, who is in you, whom you have received from God? You are not your own;"* God's children are to avoid sin and flee temptation.

3. 1st Corinthians 6:13 *"The body is not meant for sexual immorality, but for the Lord, and the Lord for the body."* Our body is to be a Temple for The Holy Spirit.

4. 1st Corinthians 6:9-10 *"Do you not know that the wicked will not inherit the kingdom of God? Do not be deceived: Neither the sexually immoral nor idolaters nor adulterers nor male prostitutes nor homosexual offenders [10]nor thieves nor the greedy nor drunkards nor slanderers nor swindlers will inherit the kingdom of God."*

5. 1st Corinthians *"We should not commit sexual immorality,*

as some of them did—and in one day twenty-three thousand of them died." Sin has consequences!

6. <u>Ephesians 6:10-18</u> *"Finally, be strong in the Lord and in his mighty power. [11]Put on the full armor of God so that you can take your stand against the devil's schemes. [12]For our struggle is not against flesh and blood, but against the rulers, against the authorities, against the powers of this dark world and against the spiritual forces of evil in the heavenly realms. [13]Therefore put on the full armor of God, so that when the day of evil comes, you may be able to stand your ground, and after you have done everything, to stand. [14]Stand firm then, with the belt of truth buckled around your waist, with the breastplate of righteousness in place, [15]and with your feet fitted with the readiness that comes from the gospel of peace. [16]In addition to all this, take up the shield of faith, with which you can extinguish all the flaming arrows of the evil one. [17]Take the helmet of salvation and the sword of the Spirit, which is the word of God. [18]And pray in the Spirit on all occasions with all kinds of prayers and requests. With this in mind, be alert and always keep on praying for all the saints.* God's children are to worship the Father in spirit and truth!

7. <u>John 4:23-24</u> *"Yet a time is coming and has now come when the true worshipers will worship the Father in the Spirit and in truth, for they are the kind of worshipers the Father seeks. [24]God is spirit, and his worshipers must worship in the Spirit and in truth."* God's children are to put on the full armor of God in order to resist the devil.

8. <u>1st Corinthians 10:13</u> *"No temptation has seized you except what is common to man. And God is faithful; he will not let you be tempted beyond what you can bear. But when you are tempted, he will also provide a way out*

so that you can stand up under it". The good news is that God will not tempt His children beyond what we can bear.

Means of Salvation

The first thing to know about "salvation" is that you have to believe that God exists and that he sent His only Son to die so that we might live forever with Him in Heaven:

1. Romans 3:22-26 *"This righteousness from God comes through faith in Jesus Christ to all who believe. There is no difference,* [23] *for all have sinned and fall short of the glory of God,* [24] *and are justified freely by his grace through the redemption that came by Christ Jesus.* [25] *God presented him as a sacrifice of atonement, through faith in his blood. He did this to demonstrate his justice, because in his forbearance he had left the sins committed beforehand unpunished* [26] *he did it to demonstrate his justice at the present time, so as to be just and the one who justifies those who have faith in Jesus."* Jesus paid the price for all our sins in full!

2. Acts 2:21 *"And everyone who calls on the name of the Lord will be saved."* Calling on God requires belief in Him and realizing that He is God and recognizing the fact that we are sinful.

3. 1st John 1:9 *"If we confess our sins, he is faithful and just and will forgive us our sins and purify us from all unrighteousness."*!

What is Repentance?

When we are sinning we are moving away from God. To repent means to "turn around", turn back toward God. Turning away from our sins and asking for forgiveness is proof of having received the Holy Spirit. Acts 2:38-39 *"Peter replied, "Repent and be baptized, every one of you, in the name of Jesus Christ for the forgiveness of your sins. And you will receive the gift of the Holy Spirit. [39]The promise is for you and your children and for all who are far off—for all whom the Lord our God will call*

Today many churches fail to mention the requirement of repentance and preach "cheap grace". These churches don't want to make someone feel guilty of their sins which may cause them to avoid attending church. True believers will not only remorse over his/her sins but also make an effort to change their behavior.

Jesus constantly preached repentance:

1. Luke 5:32 *"I have not come to call the righteous, but sinners to repentance."*

2. Luke 24:47 *"and repentance and forgiveness of sins will be preached in his name to all nations, beginning at Jerusalem."*

3. Luke 13:2 & 13:5 *"I tell you, no! But unless you repent, you too will all perish."*

Saving Others:

If we sincerely believe that those who deny Christ will spend eternity in Hell, shouldn't we make an effort to tell friends and neighbors about the Gospel? The Bible claims that we should confront other Christian believers of obvious sin so others won't follow their sinful way. 1st Timothy 5:20 *Those who sin are to be rebuked publicly, so that the others may take warning.* This is to be done only to believers and in love.

In the Old Testament man is held accountable for not warning others about sin and God's wrath:

1. Ezekiel 3:18 *"When I say to a wicked man, 'You will*

surely die,' and you do not warn him or speak out to dissuade him from his evil ways in order to save his life, that wicked man will die for his sin, and I will hold you accountable for his blood."

2. <u>Ezekiel 33:8</u> *"When I say to the wicked, 'O wicked man, you will surely die,' and you do not speak out to dissuade him from his ways, that wicked man will die for his sin, and I will hold you accountable for his blood."*

Christians are "commanded" to spread the Gospel to all who will listen. God knows who His

chosen are, those who will receive His Spirit and turn away from his/her sinful nature. Since we don't know man's heart, we are to reach out to everyone we know with the Gospel message. Only God knows His children as distinguished from Satan's children. God knows the heart whereas man only sees the outside appearance.

Conclusion

All mankind is sinful and deserves death! No matter how hard man tries, he/she is unable to "earn" his/her salvation. Man's salvation is a gift from God by His mercy and grace through faith for His Children, His chosen, His called, His elect, those appointed or predestined. It is all up to God!

CHAPTER 9

· ·

THE TRUTH WILL SET YOU FREE

Myth # 7: Being a Christian is "Easy"

Faithful Christians Will be Persecuted!

Faithful Christians are hated and persecuted by worldly antichrists", people who don't want to be reminded of their sinful nature:

1. <u>2 Timothy 3:12</u> *"In fact, everyone who wants to live a godly life in Christ Jesus will be persecuted,"*

2. <u>John 16:33</u> *"I have told you these things, so that in me you may have peace. In this world you will have trouble. But take heart! I have overcome the world."*

3. <u>John 15:19-20</u> *"If you belonged to the world, it would love you as its own. As it is, you do not belong to the world, but I have chosen you out of the world. That is why the world hates you. [20] Remember what I told you: 'A servant is not greater than his master.' If they persecuted me, they will persecute you also."*

4. Matthew 10:22 *"You will be hated by everyone because of me, but the one who stands firm to the end will be saved."*

5. 1 Peter 4:12-13 *"Dear friends, do not be surprised at the fiery ordeal that has come on you to test you, as though something strange were happening to you.*[13] *But rejoice inasmuch as you participate in the sufferings of Christ, so that you may be overjoyed when his glory is revealed."*

Christians are not to be of the world and follow man's sinful self-centered desires. God demand's to be # 1 in a Christian's life. Anything that comes before God is "Idol Worship" and God detests idol worship:

1. 1st John 2:15-16 *"Do not love the world or anything in the world. If anyone loves the world, the love of the Father is not in him.* [16] *For everything in the world—the cravings of sinful man, the lust of his eyes and the boasting of what he has and does—comes not from the Father but from the world."*

2. James 4:4 *"You adulterous people, don't you know that friendship with the world is hatred toward God? Anyone who chooses to be a friend of the world becomes an enemy of God."* Believers are not to be seduced by the world. The world distracts us from the glory of God and His commandments. Following the world is the road that leads to destruction.

3. Matthew 6:24 *"No one can serve two masters. Either you will hate the one and love the other, or you will be devoted to the one and despise the other. You cannot serve both God and money."*

People Will Turn Away From Truth

Over 1000 years ago, Timothy stated that a time would come when most people would turn their ears away from the truth and turn to myths. <u>2 Timothy 4:3-4</u> *"For the time will come when people will not put up with sound doctrine. Instead, to suit their own desires, they will gather around them a great number of teachers to say what their itching ears want to hear. ⁴ They will turn their ears away from the truth and turn aside to myths."* I believe that time has now come. This is even happening in many churches that are afraid of alienating members by telling them the truth about the challenging Christian life today. There are churches that claim that" if your faith is strong enough you will receive whatever you pray for" I call them the: *"Name it and claim it"* churches. They have fallen in to the true saying: "A church that stands for nothing will fall for anything."

Paul told believers that some people from their own group would distort the truth. <u>Acts 20:29-31</u> *"I know that after I leave, savage wolves will come in among you and will not spare the flock. ³⁰ Even from your own number men will arise and distort the truth in order to draw away disciples after them. ³¹ So be on your guard! Remember that for three years I never stopped warning each of you night and day with tears."* Paul was talking about antichrists, Satan's followers who distort the truth in an attempt to deceive us.

Did Jesus' Disciples Have an Easy life on Earth?

One would think that Jesus' closest friends, His disciples would be rewarded here on earth for all they did to help spread His Gospel message. However, all were martyred except John who died in exile. Why would we think that we deserved an easy blessed life on earth? Paul who helped spread Christianity to the gentles probably suffered the most. <u>2 Corinthians 11:23-28</u> *"I have worked much harder, been in prison more frequently, been flogged more severely, and been exposed to death again and again. ²⁴ Five times I received from the*

Jews the forty lashes minus one. [25] Three times I was beaten with rods, once I was pelted with stones, three times I was shipwrecked, I spent a night and a day in the open sea, [26] I have been constantly on the move. I have been in danger from rivers, in danger from bandits, in danger from my fellow Jews, in danger from Gentiles; in danger in the city, in danger in the country, in danger at sea; and in danger from false believers. [27] I have labored and toiled and have often gone without sleep; I have known hunger and thirst and have often gone without food; I have been cold and naked. [28] Besides everything else, I face daily the pressure of my concern for all the churches.

Even though Paul was not blessed by man's standard of blessings, he was blessed with God's Grace and God's "Peace" which passes all understanding. God even took Paul up into the 3rd Heaven for encouragement. <u>2 Corinthians 12:2</u> *"I know a man in Christ who fourteen years ago was caught up to the third heaven. Whether it was in the body or out of the body I do not know—God knows."*

Beware if Life is Going Smoothly

Being a good Christian is not an easy task. Satan will not leave you alone if you are a true Christian. If your life is going smoothly it may be a sign that you are on automatic pilot to Hell. You better get down on your knees and pray that God will show you why Satan is leaving you alone. <u>Hebrews 12:6-7</u> *"because the Lord disciplines the one he loves, and he chastens everyone he accepts as his son." [7] Endure hardship as discipline; God is treating you as his children. For what children are not disciplined by their father?"* However, God will not let us be tempted beyond what we can bear and He always gives us a way out! <u>1 Corinthians 10:13</u> *"No temptation has overtaken you except what is common to mankind. And God is faithful; he will not let you be tempted[1] beyond what you can bear. But when you are tempted, he will also provide a way out so that you can endure it.*

What did Jesus do to deserve the most humiliating, painful death imaginable? Was it because He healed the sick, made the blind see, made the deaf hear, the lame walk and fed thousands? The Jews had Jesus crucified because He claimed to be God and threatened the entire Jewish church leader's job security. Of all people, the Jewish leaders should have recognized Jesus as the promised Messiah from scriptures they studied and memorized. Today millions of Christians are persecuted just because they believe in the Bible as God's inspired Word. What harm do believers in Jesus/ God cause the world today? Does, *"loving your neighbor as yourself"* cause a problem? Which of the "10 Commandments" in injurious to society?

Sin is the world's problem and only Jesus can solve our sin problem. Jesus solved believer's sin problem by exchanging His righteousness for our sinfulness. He suffered and died in our place and took all our sins upon Himself and nailed them to the cross.

God Disciplines Those He Loves

Do you discipline your children? So does God because He loves His children. Proverbs 3:11-12 *"My son, do not despise the LORD's discipline and do not resent his rebuke, 12 because the LORD disciplines those he loves, as a father the son he delights in."* Hebrews 12:5 *"And you have forgotten that word of encouragement that addresses you as sons: "My son, do not make light of the Lord's discipline, and do not lose heart when he rebukes you."* We are to grow from God's discipline and to be thankful that He cares enough for us to correct our sinful behavior. God prunes (removes our "dead wood") so we may be more productive. John 15:2 *"He cuts off every branch in me that bears no fruit, while every branch that does bear fruit he prunes[a] so that it will be even more fruitful."*

Although no one likes to be disciplined, the Bible states that those who hate discipline lack knowledge. Proverbs 12:1 *"Whoever loves discipline loves knowledge, but he who hates correction is stupid."*

Bad Fruit = Bad Results

Jesus talks about false prophets or antichrists who distort God's word as bad fruit. No matter how much you may try and change some people, if they are antichrists, children of Satan, that's what they will remain. God has a place for such people.

1. Matthew 7:16-19 *"By their fruit you will recognize them. Do people pick grapes from thorn bushes, or figs from thistles?* [17] *Likewise, every good tree bears good fruit, but a bad tree bears bad fruit.* [18] *A good tree cannot bear bad fruit, and a bad tree cannot bear good fruit.* [19] *Every tree that does not bear good fruit is cut down and thrown into the fire."*

2. Matthew 3:10 and Luke 3:9 *"The ax is already at the root of the trees, and every tree that does not produce good fruit will be cut down and thrown into the fire."*

3. John 12:48 *"There is a judge for the one who rejects me and does not accept my words; that very word which I spoke will condemn him at the last day."* Time is running out as God has limited patience.

Those who produce good fruit are those who believe in Jesus' and try to be more like Him daily. They attempt to set a good example for others to follow. Bad fruit will not only reject God/Jesus and will try and turn others into bad fruit. also.

Are These Verses Easy to Follow?

Many demands in the Bible are impossible because of our "sin nature", we fall short of God's expectations of us. God is a jealous God and demands to be number one in our life!

He wants obedience, not just works.

God's demands may turn family members against each other. If you are doing God's work you will be persecuted as Satan will try and silence you. God also promised the peace that passes all understanding to believers. This means that even though most unbelievers would not be at peace in these circumstances, a true believer is at peace in all circumstances. This means that God comes before your spouse, your children, your possessions and your job.

1. Deuteronomy 11:32 *"be sure that you obey all the decrees and laws I am setting before you today."*

2. Matthew 5:11-12 *"Blessed are you when people insult you, persecute you and falsely say all kinds of evil against you because of me. [12] Rejoice and be glad, because great is your reward in heaven, for in the same way they persecuted the prophets who were before you."*

3. Matthew 5:44 *"But I tell you: Love your enemies and pray for those who persecute you,"*

4. Matthew 5:48 *"Be perfect, therefore, as your heavenly Father is perfect."*

5. Matthew 6:15 *"But if you do not forgive men their sins, your Father will not forgive your sins."* Hating your brother is equivalent to murder in God's eyes.

6. Matthew 7:1 *"Do not judge, or you too will be judged."* This includes thinking you are superior, smarter or better in any way than your neighbor.

7. Matthew 10:34-36 *"Do not suppose that I have come to bring peace to the earth. I did not come to bring peace, but a sword. [35] For I have come to turn a man against his father, a daughter against her mother, a daughter-in-law against her mother-in-law - [36] a man's enemies will be the members of his own household."* You are either for God or against Him. Being related to a believer carries no weight or coat tails.

8. <u>Matthew 10:37-39</u> *"Anyone who loves his father or mother more than me is not worthy of me; anyone who loves his son or daughter more than me is not worthy of me;* [38] *and anyone who does not take his cross and follow me is not worthy of me.*

9. <u>Matthew 16:24-26</u> *"Then Jesus said to his disciples, "If anyone would come after me, he must deny himself and take up his cross and follow me.* [25] *For whoever wants to save his life, will lose it, but whoever loses his life for me will find it.* [26] *What good will it be for a man if he gains the whole world, yet forfeits his soul? Or what can a man give in exchange for his soul?"*

10. <u>Matthew 19:29-30</u> *"And everyone who has left houses or brothers or sisters or father or mother or children or fields for my sake will receive a hundred times as much and will inherit eternal life.* [30] *But many who are first will be last, and many who are last will be first"*

11. <u>Mark 12:30</u> *"Love the LORD your God with all your heart and with all your soul and with all your strength."* Who can honestly say that God is always number one in their lives? This means that God comes before your spouse, your children, your possessions and your job.

12. <u>Luke 12:51-53</u> *"Do you think I came to bring peace on earth? No, I tell you, but division.* [52] *From now on there will be five in one family divided against each other, three against two and two against three.* [53] *They will be divided, father against son and son against father, mother against daughter and daughter against mother, mother-in-law against daughter-in-law and daughter-in-law against mother-in-law."*

13. <u>Luke 14:26-27</u> *"If anyone comes to me and does not hate his father and mother, his wife and children, his brothers and sisters—yes, even his own life—he cannot be my*

disciple. ²⁷*And anyone who does not carry his cross and follow me cannot be my disciple."*

14. <u>Luke 14:33</u> °*In the same way, any of you who does not give up everything he has cannot be my disciple."* The above verses are impossible for sinful man to follow. However, Jesus gives us the answer.

15. <u>John 10:38-39</u> *"and anyone who does not take his cross and follow me is not worthy of me.* ³⁹*Whoever finds his life will lose it, and whoever loses his life for my sake will find it."* Taking up your cross means being willing to sacrifice everything to accomplish God's purpose.

16. <u>1st Peter 1:15-16</u> *"But just as he who called you is holy, so be holy in all you do;* ¹⁶*for it is written: "Be holy, because I am holy."*

On our own we don't a chance of keeping God's commandments because we all sin. However, thanks for God's mercy and grace, He sent Jesus to take our place making everything possible. <u>Matthew 19:26</u> *°Jesus looked at them and said, "With man this is impossible, but with God all things are possible."*

God also promised the peace that passes all understanding to believers. This means that even though unbelievers would not be at peace in difficult circumstances, a child of God is at peace in all circumstances.

Some Things in the Bible Don't Seem Logical

Jesus stated "The last shall be first" after talking about labors hired to work in a vineyard. In this parable men who worked all day were paid the same wage as those hired at the last hour. We would say that this isn't fare but who are we to question God's generosity: <u>Matthew 20:13-16</u> *"But he answered one of them, 'Friend, I am not being unfair to you. Didn't you agree to work for a denarius?* ¹⁴*Take your pay and go. I want to give the man who was hired last the same as I gave you.* ¹⁵*Don't I have the right to do what I want with my own money? Or are you envious because I am generous?'* ¹⁶*"So the last will be first, and the first will be last."* Doesn't the creator of everything have the right to reward those He chooses?

Another quote from Jesus' parable of the talents also seems illogical to many: <u>Matthew 25: 29-30</u> *"For everyone who has will be given more, and he will have an abundance. Whoever does not have, even what he has will be taken from him.* ³⁰*And throw that worthless servant outside, into the darkness, where there will be weeping and gnashing of teeth."* This quote illustrates God's displeasure with those who don't use the talents that God has given them. I believe Jesus is talking about believers vs. non believers. The unbeliever will lose everything and spend eternity in Hell.

We Must Come to Christ as a Little Child

God also demands us to come to Him humble and as a little child. Pride is one of the things that God detests. God doesn't like anyone to take credit for blessings that He bestowed upon them:

1. <u>Matthew 18:3-4</u> *"And he said: "I tell you the truth, unless you change and become like little children, you will never enter the kingdom of heaven."*⁴*Therefore, whoever humbles himself like this child is the greatest in the kingdom of heaven.* God desires for man to have the trust as a young child has toward his parents.

2. <u>Luke 14:11</u> *"For everyone who exalts himself will be humbled, and he who humbles himself will be exalted."* Since everything comes from God, what right does anyone have to take credit for God's blessings?

Enter Through the Narrow Gate!

Most people will follow the world's broad road, the path that leads to destruction, and only a few will follow God/Jesus and put Him number one in their lives. Jesus is the narrow gate, the only way to Heaven. Matthew 7:13-14 *"Enter through the narrow gate. For wide is the gate and broad is the road that leads to destruction, and many enter through it. ¹⁴ But small is the gate and narrow the road that leads to life, and only a few find it."* Most people take the easy , self-centered path that leads to death. Matthew 22:14 *"For many are invited, but few are chosen."* Although the Christian life is inviting, only a few are chosen, called, elected, appointed or predestined and willing to follow God's law entering through the narrow gate, Jesus the Christ.

What is "Life to the Full"?

Some churches give members a false sense of security by stressing that Jesus loves everyone unconditionally giving the impression that He doesn't care how you live your life. They preach that once you become a Christians all your earthly problems will disappear. Jesus did says that he came to give believers life to the full. John 10:10 *"The thief comes only in order to steal and kill and destroy. I came that they may have and enjoy life, and have it in abundance (to the full, till it overflows).* (AMP Translation)

What does it mean to live an "abundant life"? Does an abundant life mean that all our self-centered desires will be met and God will grant all our prayers? God knows that material possessions, money, power or prestige do not bring long term happiness. If any of these items were important, why are so many wealthy, powerful people unhappy? Why do so many wealthy celebrities turn to drugs, sex and suicide?

Jesus also said that He would give us rest. Matthew 11:28 *"Come to me, all you who are weary and burdened, and I will give you rest."* The rest Jesus was talking about was His peace regardless of the stressor problems in our lives. Knowing that we will eventually spend eternity with Him in paradise gives us peace no matter what problems life throws our way.

The "abundant life" consists of "the peace that passes all understanding!" This peace is present even when times are difficult. Philippians 4:6-7 *"Do not be anxious about anything, but in everything, by prayer and petition, with thanksgiving, present your requests to God. ⁷And the peace of God, which transcends all understanding, will guard your hearts and your minds in Christ Jesus."*

True Christians shine the brightest when they are at peace even though they may suffer from a serious illness, loss of a close family member and financial stress. God's peace compensates for any personal difficulty a believer may encounter. Although the world will never be at peace but believers are at peace because they believe in God's promises in His Word.

Without God's spirit, unbelievers will never be at peace as they have no hope in their future. They believe this life on earth is as good as it gets. The elite media, the highly educated, the rich celebrities and antichrist liberals lack God's Spirit and they will never be at peace. They will die in their sins and spend eternity in Hell. Romans 8:6-7 *"The mind of sinful man is death, but the mind controlled by the Spirit is life and peace; ⁷the sinful mind is hostile to God. It does not submit to God's law, nor can it do so."* Galatians 5:22 *"But the fruit of the Spirit is love, joy, peace, patience, kindness, goodness, faithfulness,"*

Ask and You Will Receive

The following verses may give the impression that all we have to do is ask God and He will grant us our hearts desires:_

1. Matthew 7:7-8 *"Ask and it will be given to you; seek and you will find; knock and the door will be opened to you. ⁸For everyone who asks receives; he who seeks finds; and to him who knocks, the door will be opened.*

2. <u>Matthew 18:19</u> *"Again, I tell you that if two of you on earth agree about anything you ask for, it will be done for you by my Father in heaven.*

3. <u>Matthew 17:20-21</u> *He replied, "Because you have so little faith. I tell you the truth, if you have faith as small as a mustard seed, you can say to this mountain, 'Move from here to there' and it will move. Nothing will be impossible for you."*

4. <u>Matthew 21:21-22</u> *"Jesus replied, "I tell you the truth, if you have faith and do not doubt, not only can you do what was done to the fig tree, but also you can say to this mountain, 'Go, throw yourself into the sea,' and it will be done. [22] If you believe, you will receive whatever you ask for in prayer."*

How do these verses square with those of promised persecution of believers? Answered prayer is conditional of faith, and praying in God's will. If we know God's will and have His Holy Spirit, we will not ask for items of personal gratification/greed. When we ask for things that are consistent with God's will, God will answer our prayers. Sometimes God's answer is not the answer we expected, but in the long run God knows what is best for us in the long term.

What are we to do?

The first thing a seeker should do is to seek God, get to know Him, and seek His righteousness. Get into God's word and find a Bible believing church:

1. <u>Matthew 6:33</u> *"But seek first his kingdom and his righteousness, and all these things will be given to you as well."* Without God's Spirit no one will seek God. We are to turn our troubles or burdens over to Jesus.

2. Matthew 11:28-30 *"Come to me, all you who are weary and burdened, and I will give you rest.* ²⁹*Take my yoke upon you and learn from me, for I am gentle and humble in heart, and you will find rest for your souls.* ³⁰*For my yoke is easy and my burden is light."* Believers are also not to worry.

3. Matthew 6:25 *"Therefore I tell you, do not worry about your life, what you will eat or drink; or about your body, what you will wear. Is not life more important than food, and the body more important than clothes?* Jesus says that worrying about these things shows a lack of faith.

4. Matthew 6:31-32 *"So do not worry, saying, 'What shall we eat?' or 'What shall we drink?' or 'What shall we wear?'* ³²*For the pagans run after all these things, and your heavenly Father knows that you need them."* Whatever the question, Jesus is the answer!

Faith Goes Beyond Words

Christians are not to judge whether someone is saved or lost. If a person is not doing anything to help others and to promote Christian values, that person's faith is at best dead at that point in time. James, the younger brother of Jesus stated that faith without works is dead:

1. James 1:22 *"Do not merely listen to the word, and so deceive yourselves. Do what it says."* James, the brother of Jesus went on to says to do what it says.

2. James 2:14-17 *"What good is it, my brothers and sisters, if someone claims to have faith but has no deeds? Can such faith save them?* ¹⁵ *Suppose a brother or a sister is without clothes and daily food.* ¹⁶ *If one of you says to them, "Go in peace; keep warm and well fed," but does nothing about their physical needs, what good is it?* ¹⁷

In the same way, faith by itself, if it is not accompanied by action, is dead." Those having faith in God/Jesus, will seek God through prayer and His Word and do what it says.

3. James 2:24 *"You see that a person is considered righteous by what they do and not by faith alone"*

4. James 2:26 *"As the body without the spirit is dead, so faith without deeds is dead."* James is not saying that you can earn your way into heaven, rather that talk is cheap. True believers do good works out of thanksgiving for what God has done for them not to earn their salvation. God knows man's heart, your motives.

5. James 2:20 *"You foolish person, do you want evidence that faith without deeds is useless?"*

James does not contradict that we are saved by grace through faith. James believes there should be evidence of one's saving faith. Remember that we were "created in Christ Jesus to do good works, which God prepared in advance for us to do. Ephesians 2:10 *"For we are God's workmanship, created in Christ Jesus to do good works, which God prepared in advance for us to do."* Acts of righteousness will be lost if done to gain attention from your fellow man. Matthew 6:1 *"Be careful not to do your 'acts of righteousness' before men, to be seen by them. If you do, you will have no reward from your Father in heaven.""*

Are their Rewards for Good Works?

Yes, there are rewards for works done while here on earth: Although, God's children will be persecuted, they will also be rewarded in Heaven. We are to work with all our heart in whatever we do as if God was our boss.

1. Matthew 16:27 *"For the Son of Man is going to come in his Father's glory with his angels, and then he will*

reward each person according to what he has done." Righteousness will also be rewarded.

2. Ephesians 6:8 *"because you know that the Lord will reward each one for whatever good they do, whether they are slave or free."* God knows our heart and even our thoughts and rewards us according to our conduct.

3. Colossians 3:23 *"Whatever you do, work at it with all your heart, as working for the Lord, not for men,"*

4. Psalm 62:12 *"and that you, O Lord, are loving. Surely you will reward each person according to what he has done."*

5. Proverbs 11:18 *"The wicked man earns deceptive wages, but he who sows righteousness reaps a sure reward."*

6. Proverbs 13:21 *"Misfortune pursues the sinner, but prosperity is the reward of the righteous."*

7. Proverbs 19:17 *"He who is kind to the poor lends to the LORD, and he will reward him for what he has done." Man will also be rewarded for helping his enemy.*

8. Proverbs 25:21-22 *"If your enemy is hungry, give him food to eat; if he is thirsty, give him water to drink.* [22] *In doing this, you will heap burning coals on his head, and the LORD will reward you."*

9. Jeremiah 17:10 *"I the LORD search the heart and examine the mind, to reward a man according to his conduct, according to what his deeds deserve."*

There are rewards in Heaven but "works" will not help you earn your way there. Man is not saved by works but is a gift from God through faith.

Being a Christian Requires Faith and doing God's Will!

When Jesus comes back to judge the world, separate the lost from the saved, many people will be gravely disappointed when He sends them away claiming that He doesn't know them.

Matthew 7:21-27 *"Not everyone who says to me, 'Lord, Lord,' will enter the kingdom of heaven, but only the one who does the will of my Father who is in heaven." Many will say to me on that day, 'Lord, Lord, did we not prophesy in your name and in your name drive out demons and in your name perform many miracles?'* [23] *Then I will tell them plainly, 'I never knew you. Away from me, you evildoers!'* [24] *"Therefore everyone who hears these words of mine and puts them into practice is like a wise man who built his house on the rock.* [25] *The rain came down, the streams rose, and the winds blew and beat against that house; yet it did not fall, because it had its foundation on the rock.* [26] *But everyone who hears these words of mine and does not put them into practice is like a foolish man who built his house on sand.* [27] *The rain came down, the streams rose, and the winds blew and beat against that house, and it fell with a great crash."*

It is much easier to be worldly and just go along with the crowd. Life may go on smoothly as Satan will leave you alone as you are probably on an automatic pathway to Hell. Today Christians are persecuted in higher numbers than any other religious group worldwide. In the United Stated Christianity is the only religious group that is constantly ridiculed on TV and by the mainline media and by Hollywood.

Conclusion:

Being a Christian is not easy but the eternal benefits are well worth the effort!

CHAPTER 10

THE TRUTH WILL SET YOU FREE

Myth # 8: "Fearing" God Means "Respect"

Definition of Fear vs. Respect

Many Christians believe that when the Bible says to "fear" God, it actually only to respect or be in "awe" of Him. This notion of "respect" has been reinforced by many churches today in order to downplay God's just wrath. They mainly want to focus on God's unconditional love which is elaborated on in chapter five. Webster's Dictionary defines fear as: *"a distressing emotion aroused by appending pain, danger, evil, etc., whether real or imagined; the feeling or condition of being afraid".* Contrast this with the definition of "respect": *"esteem for or a sense of the worth or excellence of a person, a personal quality or trait, or something considered as a manifestation of a personal quality or trait."* The following Hebrew's passage fits the definition of fear perfectly. Hebrews 12:21 *"The sight was so terrifying that Moses said, "I am trembling with fear."*

Fearing God is Wise and Essential for Faith

God uses the "carrot and stick" approach to reach man. The carrot is salvation through Christ's forgiveness of all our sins and the stick is fear of God's power over where we will spend eternity. Being afraid of God illustrates believer's wisdom and knowledge of a powerful God.

1. Deuteronomy 6:13 *"Fear the LORD your God, serve him only and take your oaths in his name."*

2. Deuteronomy 12:13 *"And now, O Israel, what does the LORD your God ask of you but to fear the LORD your God, to walk in all his ways, to love him, to serve the LORD your God with all your heart and with all your soul,"*

3. 1 Samuel 12:24 *"But be sure to fear the LORD and serve him faithfully with all your heart; consider what great things he has done for you."*

4. Psalm 86:11 *"Teach me your way, O LORD, and I will walk in your truth; give me an undivided heart, that I may fear your name."* Knowing God's power/wrath and His aversion to sin puts the fear of punishment in the minds of believers not wanting to spend eternity in hell.

5. Psalms *111:10* *"The fear of the LORD is the beginning of wisdom; all who follow his precepts have good understanding. To him belongs eternal praise"*

6. Proverbs 1:7 *"The fear of the LORD is the beginning of knowledge, but fools despise wisdom and discipline."*

7. Philippians 2:12 *"Therefore, my dear friends, as you have always obeyed—not only in my presence, but now much more in my absence—continue to work out your salvation with fear and trembling"*

8. Ecclesiastes 12:13 *"Now all has been heard; here is*

> *the conclusion of the matter: Fear God and keep his*
> *commandments, for this is the whole duty of man."*

9. Not only are we to be afraid of God's Almighty power, but
    we are to hold Him in "awe" for all of His blessings, His
    mercy and His grace,.

Angels Calmed People's Fears

Every time an angel appeared in the Bible the first thing the angel would
say was not to be fear him. Luke 1:30 *"But the angel said to her, "Do*
not be afraid, Mary, you have found favor with God." Mary was
frightened by the appearance of God's Angel. The angel that appeared
to Mary was telling her not to respect him. Isaiah 41:10 *"So do not*
fear, for I am with you; do not be dismayed, for I am your God. I
will strengthen you and help you;"

Fear God not Man!

There is no doubt that we should respect God/Jesus and hold Him in
awe because God/Jesus is the creator and sustainer of the universe. We
should also fear God because of His aversion to sin and its conquest
for unbelievers/antichrists.

1. Deuteronomy 31:12 *"Assemble the people—men, women*
    and children, and the foreigners residing in your towns—
    so they can listen and learn to fear the Lord your God
    and follow carefully all the words of this law.

2. Deuteronomy 32:22 *"For a fire will be kindled by my*
    wrath, one that burns down to the realm of the dead
    below. It will devour the earth and its harvests and set
    afire the foundations of the mountains."

3. Deuteronomy 32:35 *"It is mine to avenge; I will repay.*

> *In due time their foot will slip their day of disaster is near and their doom rushes upon them."*

4. Psalm 27-1 *"The LORD is my light and my salvation— whom shall I fear? The LORD is the stronghold of my life—of whom shall I be afraid?"*

5. Psalm 76:7 *"You alone are to be feared. Who can stand before you when you are angry?"*

6. Psalm 90:11 *"Who knows the power of your anger? For your wrath is as great as the fear that is due you."*

7. Psalm 96:9 *"Worship the LORD in the splendor of his holiness; tremble before him, all the earth."*

8. Isaiah 8:13 *"The LORD Almighty is the one you are to regard as holy, he is the one you are to fear, he is the one you are to dread,"*

Unbelievers are more concerned with pleasing man than pleasing God. No matter what happens to God's children here on their brief time earth, they will spend eturnity with Him in Heaven.

Blessings and Peace for Fearing God

God's children who fear and obey God lack nothing. Psalm 34:9 *"Fear the LORD, you his saints, for those who fear him lack nothing."* Psalm 46:2 *"Therefore we will not fear, though the earth give way and the mountains fall into the heart of the sea"* God promises blessings for those who fear Him.

1. Psalm 112:1 *"Blessed is the man who fears the LORD, who finds great delight in his commands."*

2. Psalm 112:7-8 *"He will have no fear of bad news; his heart is steadfast, trusting in the LORD. ⁸ His heart is secure, he will have no fear; in the end he will look in triumph*

on his foes." Righteous and God fearing men will not only be blessed but they will be fearless when trouble comes.

3. Psalm 128:1 *"Blessed are all who fear the LORD, who walk in his ways."*

4. Psalm 128:4 *"Thus is the man blessed who fears the LORD."*

5. Psalm 130:3-4 *"If you, O LORD, kept a record of sins, O Lord, who could stand? ⁴ But with you there is forgiveness; therefore you are feared."*

6. Psalm 145:19 *"He fulfills the desires of those who fear him; he hears their cry and saves them"*

7. Proverbs 19:23 *"The fear of the LORD leads to life: Then one rests content, untouched by trouble."* Fearing God actually brings peace.

8. Isaiah 33:6 *"He will be the sure foundation for your times, a rich store of salvation and wisdom and knowledge; the fear of the LORD is the key to this treasure.*

God was able to bring a sense of peace to me and my wife in spite a severe near death accident, months of hospitalization, bankruptcy and loss of our home of 24 years. Chapter two, "Why Me God", describes in detail of what I went through after my severe accident. It took several years to worked things out but eventually it strengthen me physically, financially and spiritually.

God Commands us to Fear Him and Obey Him

Man's job here on earth is to serve God, keep His commandments and fear His power of eternal life or eternal death over us! Additional verses relation to fearing God:

1. Deuteronomy 6:13 *"Fear the LORD your God, serve him only and take your oaths in his name."*

2. Deuteronomy 31:12-13 *"Assemble the people—men, women and children, and the aliens living in your towns—so they can listen and learn to fear the LORD your God and follow carefully all the words of this law."* [13] *Their children, who do not know this law, must hear it and learn to fear the LORD your God as long as you live in the land you are crossing the Jordan to possess."*

3. Joshua 4:24 *"He did this so that all the peoples of the earth might know that the hand of the LORD is powerful and so that you might always fear the LORD your God."* We are to fear God's power!

4. Joshua 24:14 *"Now fear the LORD and serve him with all faithfulness. Throw away the gods your forefathers worshiped beyond the River and in Egypt, and serve the LORD."*

5. Psalms 2:11 *"Serve the LORD with fear and rejoice with trembling."*

6. Psalm 19:9 *"The fear of the LORD is pure, enduring forever. The ordinances of the LORD are sure and altogether righteous."*

7. Psalm 33:8 *"Let all the earth fear the LORD; let all the people of the world revere him."* This verse indicate both respect as well as fear.

Conclusion:

The above Bible verses clearly that "to fear God" is not just respect, but additionally an emotion of being afraid of His awesome sovereign power. Yes, it is important to hold God in "awe" but we are also to fear

God/Jesus due to His justified potential wrath. Fearing God will result in "knowledge, wisdom, rewards and peace". When you fear God you will have nothing else to fear. Fearing God indicates your knowledge that: "God is God and you are not"!

CHAPTER 11

THE TRUTH WILL SET YOU FREE

Myth # 9: The Saints Raptured Pre-Tribulation

The Rapture Occurs After the Great Tribulation.

Another myth is that Christians are raptured, taken to meet Jesus in the air, before the "Great Tribulation". The seven year Great Tribulation is going to be a horrific time on earth prior to Christ's return. Danial in 600 B.C. wrote about the end times when Satan and his followers would rule the world:

1. Daniel 7:21-22 *"As I watched, this horn was <u>waging war against the holy people and defeating them,</u> ²² until the Ancient of Days came and pronounced judgment in favor of the holy people of the Most High, and the time came when they possessed the kingdom".* God's holy people were being defeated so they must be present during the tribulation period..

2. Daniel 8:24-25 *"He will become very strong, but not by*

his own power. He will cause astounding devastation and will succeed in whatever he does. <u>He will destroy those who are mighty, the holy people.</u> [25] *He will cause deceit to prosper, and he will consider himself superior. When they feel secure, he will destroy many and take his stand against the Prince of princes. Yet he will be destroyed, but not by human power."* Jesus is the Prince of princes and God wins in the end.

3. <u>Daniel 9:13-14</u> "*Just as it is written in the Law of Moses, all this disaster has come on us, yet we have not sought the favor of the Lord our God by turning from our sins and giving attention to your truth.* [14] *The Lord did not hesitate to bring the disaster on us, for the Lord our God is righteous in everything he does; yet we have not obeyed him".* There are and were consequences for disobedience.

4. <u>Daniel 9:36</u> "*The king will do as he pleases. He will exalt and magnify himself above every god and will say unheard-of things against the God of gods. <u>He will be successful until the time of wrath is completed,</u> for what has been determined must take place."* God's will not be thwarted.

5. <u>Daniel 12:1-2</u> "*At that time Michael, the great prince who protects your people, will arise. <u>There will be a time of distress such as has not happened from the beginning of nations until then.</u> But at that time your people—everyone whose name is found written in the book—will be delivered.* [2] *Multitudes who sleep in the dust of the earth will awake: some to everlasting life, others to shame and everlasting contempt."* There is a day of judgement for everyone both dead and alive. We are living in the last days but no one knows when" judgement day" will arrive.

About 2000 Years later John wrote Revelations

Revelations gives more detail than Daniel but both indicate that believers are present during the Great Tribulation. Although Revelations is difficult to follow it is the only book in the Bible that offers a blessing for those who read/hear the prophecy and take it to heart. Revelations 1:3 *"Blessed is the one who reads aloud the words of this prophecy, and blessed are those who hear it and take to heart what is written in it, because the time is near."*

In Revelations, John paints a pretty grim picture of what happens to all living things on earth during that 7 year tribulation period. John's vision about the last days:

1. Revelation 6:4 *"Then another horse came out, a fiery red one. Its rider was given power to take peace from the earth and to make people kill each other. To him was given a large sword."*

2. Revelation 6:8 *"I looked, and there before me was a pale horse! Its rider was named Death, and Hades was following close behind him. They were given power over a fourth of the earth to kill by sword, famine and plague, and by the wild beasts of the earth."*

3. Revelation 6:10-11 *"**They called out in a loud voice, "How long, Sovereign Lord, holy and true, until you judge the inhabitants of the earth and avenge our blood? 11 Then each of them was given a white robe, and they were told to wait a little longer, until the number of their fellow servants and brothers who were to be killed as they had been was completed.""*** This indicates that God's children are present during the tribulation period.

4. Revelation 7:3 *"Do not harm the land or the sea or the trees until we put a seal on the foreheads of the servants of our God."* God's people were present during the Great Tribulation waiting for His seal on their foreheads.

5. Revelation 7:14 "I *answered, "Sir, you know."And he said, "These are they who have come out of the great tribulation; they have washed their robes and made them white in the blood of the Lamb."* The saints came out of the great tribulation and washed their robes in Jesus' blood.

6. Revelation 9:4 "*They were told not to harm the grass of the earth or any plant or tree, but only those people who did not have the seal of God on their foreheads."* **God protected the saints here so they must have been present.**

7. Revelation 9:6 "*During those days people will seek death but will not find it; they will long to die, but death will elude them."*

8. Revelation 12:7-8 " *Then war broke out in heaven. Michael and his angels fought against the dragon, and the dragon and his angels fought back.* [8] *But he was not strong enough, and they lost their place in heaven."* Satan, the dragon, won this battle but the war was not over.

9. Revelation 13:7-8 "*It was given power to wage war against God's holy people and to conquer them. And it was given authority over every tribe, people, language and nation. All inhabitants of the earth will worship the beast—all whose names have not been written in the Lamb's book of life, the Lamb who was slain from the creation of the world.* Again God's people were there.

10. Revelation 13:16-17 "*It also forced all people, great and small, rich and poor, free and slave, to receive a mark on their right hands or on their foreheads,[17] so that they could not buy or sell unless they had the mark, which is the name of the beast or the number of its name."*

11. Revelations 14:12 "*And the smoke of their torment rises for ever and ever. There is no rest day or night for those who worship the beast and his image, or for anyone who receives the mark of his name."* [12]*This calls for patient*

endurance on the part of the saints who obey God's commandments and remain faithful to Jesus." I believe this is part of the tribulation illustrating that Christians are present during the tribulation.

12. Revelations 20:4-5 *"And I saw the souls of those who had been beheaded because of their testimony about Jesus and because of the word of God. They had not worshiped the beast or its image and had not received its mark on their foreheads or their hands. They came to life and reigned with Christ a thousand years."* Again those who were beheaded because of Christ were present and martyred during the tribulation period. The rest of the dead did not come to life until the thousand years were ended. This is the first resurrection. Verse 6 goes on to say *"The second death has no power over them, but they will be priests of God and of Christ and will reign with him for a thousand years."*

Jewish religious leaders during Jesus' time looked for a "quick fix" to resolve the Roman occupation. They believed in a conquering warrior like King David who would restore Israel to its glory and power under King David and King Solomon. They disregarded all the Old Testament prophecies regarding a "suffering servant. Israel/Jews suffered greatly in 70 AD when the temple was destroyed. God's chosen people are still persecuted today.

The Rapture...Meeting Jesus in the Air

No one would want to be alive and suffer through the Great Tribulation. Man's solution to the problem is to believe the saints are raptured there by avoiding that dreadful time. The same may be said for those who believe that God loves everyone unconditionally therefore disobedience and a lack of faith to God's law has no consequences. The God of our creation is much easier to satisfy than the true God of the Bible! **A at** quote at BSF, Bible Study Fellowship, regarding the time of the rapture: *"be prepared for an after, "a post tribulation rapture but hope for a before, "a pretribulation rapture".*

It is wishful thinking on the part of man by believing that Christians can avoid the agony of living through the 7 year tribulation period. Although the word "rapture" is never mentioned in the Bible, the Bible talks about a time when Christians are taken instantly out of the world to meet Jesus in the air:

1. Matthew 24:30-31 *"Then will appear the sign of the Son of Man in heaven. And then all the peoples of the earth will mourn when they see the Son of Man coming on the clouds of heaven, with power and great glory. And he will send his angels with a loud trumpet call, and they will gather his elect from the four winds, from one end of the heavens to the other."* I believe this is post tribulation.

2. 1 Thessalonians 4:16-17 *"For the Lord himself will come down from heaven, with a loud command, with the voice of the archangel and with the trumpet call of God, and the dead in Christ will rise first.* [17] *After that, we who are still alive and are left will be caught up together with them in the clouds to meet the Lord in the air. And so we will be with the Lord forever."* Again could be post tribulation.

3. 1 Corinthians 15:51-54 *"Listen, I tell you a mystery: We will not all sleep, but we will all be changed—* [52] *in a flash, in the twinkling of an eye, at the last trumpet. For the trumpet will sound, the dead will be raised imperishable, and we will be changed.* [53] *For the perishable must clothe itself with the imperishable, and the mortal with immortality.* [54] *When the perishable has been clothed with the imperishable, and the mortal with immortality, then the saying that is written will come true: "Death has been swallowed up in victory."*

4. <u>1 Corinthians 15:22-26</u> *"For as in Adam all die, so in Christ all will be made alive. ²³ But each in turn: Christ, the firstfruits; then, when he comes, those who belong to him. ²⁴ Then the end will come, when he hands over the kingdom to God the Father after he has destroyed all dominion, authority and power.²⁵ For he must reign until he has put all his enemies under his feet.²⁶ The last enemy to be destroyed is death.*

If any group of people should have been rewarded for their faith it would seem logical that Jesus' disciples and close friends would be at the top of the list. However, all His disciples were persecuted and all except John were martyred. The apostle Paul suffered but God said His grace was sufficient which made Paul stronger. These examples of suffering here on earth, leads me to believe that the rapture takes place after the "great tribulation" and the Millennium, the 1000 year reign of Christ.

Who was Taken in the Matthew & Luke Passages?

The belief that man is raptured prior to the tribulation period is disputed by scripture. Two bible verses where readers get this misconception originate from:

1. <u>Matthew 24:38-40</u> *"For in the days before the flood, people were eating and   drinking, marrying and giving in marriage, up to the day Noah entered the ark; ³⁹ and they knew nothing about what would happen until the flood came and took them all away. That is how it will be at the coming of the Son of Man. ⁴⁰ Two men will be in the field; one will be taken and the other left. ⁴¹ Two women will be grinding with a hand mill; one will be taken and the other left."* A similar passage is found in:

2. <u>Luke 17:34-37</u> *"I tell you, on that night two people will be in one bed; one will be taken and the other left. ³⁵ Two women will be grinding grain together; one will be taken and the other left."*

[37]*"Where, Lord?" they asked. He replied, "Where there is a dead body, there the vultures will gather."*

The above verses talk about two groups of people that are separated from each other. **We are led to believe that those "taken" are the Saints and going to meet Christ in the air.** The *"Left Behind"* Book Series made millions of dollars elaborating on this false concept. However, **the Bible indicates that those who were taken were actually the wicked majority not righteous Noah and his family who was left behind on earth.** Genesis 6:11-13 *"Now the earth was corrupt in God's sight and was full of violence.* [12] *God saw how corrupt the earth had become, for all the people on earth had corrupted their ways.* [13] *So God said to Noah, "I am going to put an end to all people, for the earth is filled with violence because of them. I am surely going to destroy both them and the earth."* In the Genesis passage, God was referring to the time of the great flood where **it was sinful man not believers who were taken by the great flood. Noah and his family remained on earth while all the unbelievers were taken by the flood and killed.**

In the Luke passage, Jesus' disciple asked Him "where would they be taken" and Jesus' response was a *"Where there is a dead body, there the vultures will gather."* This is not a description of Heaven but more indicative of Hell! Matthew 13:41-42 *"The Son of Man will send out his angels, and they will weed out of his kingdom everything that causes sin and all who do evil.* [42] *They will throw them into the fiery furnace, where there will be weeping and gnashing of teeth."* **Both passages indicate that those who were taken were not God's children and Heaven was not their destination!**

If the rapture occurred prior to the great tribulation, the people mentioned would not have suffered beheading's, because of their testimony about Jesus. This proves that believers were present throughout the tribulation period.

During the great tribulation period many of the Saints were persecuted and put to death. Those saints who stood firm throughout this period and those martyred were saved. Matthew 24:9-13 *"Then you will be handed over to be persecuted and put to death, and you will be hated by all nations because of me.* 10 *At that time many will turn away from the faith and will betray and hate each other,* **11** *and many false prophets will appear and deceive many people.* **12** *Because of the increase of wickedness, the love of most will grow cold,* **13** *but the one who stands firm to the end will be saved."* I believe Jesus is talking about the Great Tribulation

God knows His children, those who will persevere. Matthew 24:22-24 *"If those days had not been cut short, no one would survive, but for the sake of the elect those days will be shortened.* **23** *At that time if anyone says to you, 'Look, here is the Messiah!' or, 'There he is!' do not believe it.* **24** *For false messiahs and false prophets will appear and perform great signs and wonders to deceive, if possible, even the elect."* **Why would God cut short the tribulation period if the Saints were already with Him in Heaven? Why would Jesus warn them about false messiah's appearing performing great signs and wonders to deceive even the elect if the saints were raptured?**

God Gives Satan Power Over the Saints

For some reason, that only God knows, Satan is given power to conquer the Saints. However, God is still in control and loss of life on earth is nothing when compared to eternity with Him in heaven. Revelations 12:17 *"Then the dragon was enraged at the woman and went off to wage war against the rest of her offspring—those who keep God's commands and hold fast their testimony about Jesus."* Revelations 13:7-8 *"It was given power to wage war against God's holy people and to conquer them. And it was given authority over every tribe, people, language and nation.* **8** *All inhabitants of the earth will worship the beast—all whose names have not been written in the Lamb's book of life, the Lamb who was slain from the creation of the world."* **Who would Satan wage war with if "God's holy people were already raptured?**

Revelations 7:13-14 *"Then one of the elders asked me, "These in white robes—who are they, and where did they come from?"* **John answered** *"And he said, "These are they who have come out of the* *great tribulation; they have washed their robes and made them* *white in the blood of the Lamb."* **Again I believe this is further** **proof that the saints are not raptured prior to the great tribulation**.

Those who were martyred cry out. <u>Revelations 6:10-11</u> *"They called* *out in a loud voice, "How long, Sovereign Lord, holy and true,* *until you judge the inhabitants of the earth and avenge our blood?"* Although many saints will lose their life during the great tribulation, they will be with God forever in Heaven. <u>Luke 17:33</u> *"Whoever tries to* *keep their life will lose it, and whoever loses their life will preserve* *it."* <u>Revelations 14:12</u> *"This calls for patient endurance on the part* *of the people of God who keep his commands and remain faithful* *to Jesus."* Those who stand firm and resist Satan will be rewarded. <u>Revelations 3:21</u> *"To the one who is victorious, I will give the right* *to sit with me on my throne, just as I was victorious and sat down* *with my Father on his throne."*

Only God knows when His final judgment will occur and who His true children are.

The above verses clearly indicate that Christians are not raptured prior to the tribulation but they are present throughout the tribulation period. Therefore they are persecuted for seven years, then rewarded for their suffering and for standing firm by not worshiping the beast.

The 1000 Year Reign of Christ

Many theologians disagree on when the 1000 year reign of Christ takes place and if the time is literally 1000 years. Weather Christ's reign is actually 1000 years or a "long period of time" is irrelevant. What is important is when it takes place and what happens during that time period. Revelations chapter 20 mentions an angle coming out of heaven and bounding up Satan for 1000 years. <u>Revelations 20:2-3</u> *"He seized* *the dragon, that ancient serpent, who is the devil, or Satan, and* *bound him for a thousand years.* [3] *He threw him into the Abyss,* *and locked and sealed it over him, to keep him from deceiving the* *nations anymore until the thousand years were ended. After that, he must be set free for a short time."* Note that Satan is only imprisoned for a period of time and not sent to Hell yet.

After Satan and his followers are removed from earth, Jesus begins his 1000 year reign of peace on earth. I believe this is what the Matthew and Luke passages mentioned earlier in this chapter referred to. They are removed just as the sinful people were taken in the time of Noah. True peace could only happen when Satan and his children were removed from the earth.

Now those martyrs killed during the tribulation, those who did not worship the beast, will come back to life and reign with Christ for a 1000 years or a long period of time. Revelations 20:4-5 *"__They came to life and reigned with Christ a thousand years. 5 (The rest of the dead did not come to life until the thousand years were ended.) This is the first resurrection." "The second death has no power over them, but they will be priests of God and of Christ and will reign with him for a thousand years."__*

Jesus then comes in his glory and separates the saints from the sinners. Matthew 25:31-32 *"When the Son of Man comes in his glory, and all the angels with him, he will sit on his glorious throne. 32 All the nations will be gathered before him, and he will separate the people one from another as a shepherd separates the sheep from the goats. 33 He will put the sheep on his right and the goats on his left. 34 "Then the King will say to those on his right, '__Come, you who are blessed by my Father; take your inheritance, the kingdom prepared for you since the creation of the world."__* Matthew 25:41 *"Then he will say to those on his left, 'Depart from me, you who are cursed, into the eternal fire prepared for the devil and his angels."*

Sequence of Events

It is my understanding that the sequence of events in Revelations is:

1. "The Great Tribulation" …A seven year period of Hell on earth.

2. "The Millennium", Christ's' 1000 Year Reign"… Complete peace on earth.

3. "God's Judgment" …The end of the world.

It is obvious to me from the above passages that Christ's 1000 year reign and the "great tribulation" hasn't happened to date. Also obvious, is that the saints, God's children are present during the great tribulation and many are martyred during that period. Satan must be bound up and removed from deceiving the nations in order for Christ's peaceful reign to occur. The 1000 year peace also could not occur until Satan and his evil children were removed from earth. Therefore, those "taken" in the Matthew and Luke verses are those removed from earth so peace could occur during Christ's reign. Matthew 13:41-43 *"The Son of Man will send out his angels, and they will weed out of his kingdom everything that causes sin and all who do evil. 42 They will throw them into the blazing furnace, where there will be weeping and gnashing of teeth. 43 Then the righteous will shine like the sun in the kingdom of their Father. Whoever has ears, let them hear."*

Events Leading Up to the Final Judgment

Christians today believe that Jesus is now sitting at the right hand of God in Heaven and some day He will return to earth. Revelations indicates that Christ returns for His 1000 year reign, the Millennium, after the great tribulation. Christ rewards those loyal to Him, those martyred through the tribulation, by raising them from the dead. They will reign with Him as priests of God throughout the Millennium. Christ's 1000 year reign ends when Satan is released from the Abyss for a short time which is the beginning of Armageddon, where Satan is thrown into the fiery lake of burning sulfur where he and his followers will be tormented day and night for ever and ever. Revelations 20:10 *"And the devil, who deceived them, was thrown into the lake of burning sulfur, where the beast and the false prophet had been thrown. They will be tormented day and night for ever and ever."*

The Final Judgment

The rapture occurs at the final judgment, the end of the world as we know it. At that time believers will be changed in an instant and given imperishable bodies. The dead will be raised 1st and the rest of the believers will meet Jesus in the air. The children of Satan will be judged and sent to eternal punishment where Satan is thrown into the fiery lake of burning sulfur where he and his followers will be tormented day and night for ever and ever. <u>Revelations 11:18</u> *"The nations were angry, and your wrath has come. The time has come for judging the dead, and for rewarding your servants the prophets and your people who revere your name, both great and small— and for destroying those who destroy the earth."* Matthew 24:30-31 *"At that time the sign of the Son of Man will appear in the sky, and all the nations of the earth will mourn. They will see the Son of Man coming on the clouds of the sky, with power and great glory.* ^{31}*And he will send his angels with a loud trumpet call, and they will gather his elect from the four winds, from one end of the heavens to the other."*

Hell is not a place where you want to spend eternity! <u>Revelations 14:11-12</u> *"they, too, will drink the wine of God's fury, which has been poured full strength into the cup of his wrath. They will be tormented with burning sulfur in the presence of the holy angels and of the Lamb.* ^{11} *And the smoke of their torment will rise for ever and ever. There will be no rest day or night for those who worship the beast and its image, or for anyone who receives the mark of its name."*

The Dead are Judged

The dead are judged and all unbelievers, the children of Satan are sent to Hell. <u>Revelations 20:12-15</u> *"And I saw the dead, great and small, standing before the throne, and books were opened. Another book was opened, which is the book of life. The dead were judged according to what they had done as recorded in the books.* ^{13} *The sea gave up the dead that were in it, and death and Hades gave up the dead that were in them, and each person was judged according to what they had done.* [14] *Then death and Hades were thrown into the lake of fire. The lake of fire is the second death.* [15] *Anyone whose name was not found written in the book of life was thrown into the lake of fire."* Revelations 21:8 *"But the cowardly, the unbelieving, the vile, the murderers, the sexually immoral, those who practice magic arts, the idolaters and all liars—they will be consigned to the fiery lake of burning sulfur. This is the second death."*

God's children will be taken into Heaven where they will be with the Lord forever. Revelations 21:3-4 *"And I heard a loud voice from the throne saying, "Look! God's dwelling place is now among the people, and he will dwell with them. They will be his people, and God himself will be with them and be their God.* [4], *He will wipe every tear from their eyes. There will be no more death' or mourning or crying or pain, for the old order of things has passed away."*

Last the earth and the heavens will be completely destroyed. Revelations 21:1-2 *"Then I saw "a new heaven and a new earth, for the first heaven and the first earth had passed away, and there was no longer any sea.* [2] *I saw the Holy City, the new Jerusalem, coming down out of heaven from God, prepared as a bride beautifully dressed for her husband."*

Everyone Will Live Forever Somewhere

Whether you are a believer or a denier of Christ, you will live forever. The difference is where you will spend eternity either in Heaven or in Hell. In heaven there is total peace where love abounds and there is an absence of sickness and sadness. Hell is reserved for Satan and his children/antichrist. It is a place where one burns eternally but never dies. Remember how it feels when you burn your finger? I can't imagine having my whole body burned forever and ever without any relief. Revelations 20:14 *"Then death and Hades were thrown into the lake of fire. The lake of fire is the second death.* [15] *Anyone whose name was not found written in the book of life was thrown into the lake of fire."*

Conclusion

I believe that all Christians want an easy painless way out of life. No one likes discipline or struggles in life. We like our creature comforts and don't want to suffer or make unnecessary sacrifices. Maybe that is why the "Rapture" pre tribulation myth is so appealing. However the bible tells a different story of suffering and sacrifice: Matthew 10:37 *"Anyone who loves their father or mother more than me is not worthy of me; anyone who loves their son or daughter more than me is not worthy of me. 38 Whoever does not take up their cross and follow me is not worthy of me. 39 Whoever finds their life will lose it, and whoever loses their life for my sake will find it."* Matthew 17:24-27 *"Then Jesus said to his disciples, "Whoever wants to be my disciple must deny themselves and take up their cross and follow me. 25 For whoever wants to save their life will lose it, but whoever loses their life for me will find it. 26 What good will it be for someone to gain the whole world, yet forfeit their soul? Or what can anyone give in exchange for their soul? 27 For the Son of Man is going to come in his Father's glory with his angels, and then he will reward each person according to what they have done."* God and His children win and Satan and all antichrist's lose!

"With God help all things are possible". No matter what happens to us on earth, weather you live to be 110 years old or die at 10 years of age, it is just a drop in the ocean compared to eternity. God knows His children and our sinful nature, that is why He sent His only Son to seek and save the lost. Luke 19:10 *"For the Son of Man came to seek and to save the lost."*

CHAPTER # 12

....

THE TRUTH WILL SET YOU FREE

Myth # 10: The Bible is Against Capital Punishment

The Bible is Against Murder not Killing!

Throughout the Old Testament, God commanded His people to kill His enemies and purge evil/sin from the land. This included the killing of men, women and children that He wanted eliminated from the earth:

1. Deuteronomy 20:16-17 *"**However, in the cities of the nations the Lord your God is giving you as an inheritance, do not leave alive anything that breathes.** [17] **Completely destroy**[a] **them—the Hittites, Amorites, Canaanites, Perizzites, Hivites and Jebusites—as the LORD your God has commanded you.**_*

2. 1 Samuel 2-3 *"**This is what the Lord Almighty says: 'I will punish the Amalekites for what they did to Israel when they waylaid them as they came up from Egypt.** [3] **Now go, attack the Amalekites and totally destroy**[a] **all that***

belongs to them. Do not spare them; put to death men and women, children and infants, cattle and sheep, camels and donkeys".

3. <u>1st Samuel 15:19</u> *"And he sent you on a mission, saying, 'Go and completely destroy those wicked people, the Amalekites; make war on them until you have wiped them out.'"*

The Bible actually says: <u>Exodus 20:13</u> *"You shall not murder."* However, God's commandment distinguishes between killing and murder. In all Bible translations except for the <u>"King James Version"</u> They use the word murder rather than kill. The Roman Catholics church and some Christian denominations still teach that the commandment means to not "kill" any human being. Killing in wartime and for self-defense has been accepted throughout history. God has commanded killing in order purge evil from the land.

C.S. Lewis had the best explanation of killing in war vs. murder. *"Does loving your enemy mean not punishing him? No, for loving myself does not mean that I ought not to subject myself to punishment—even to death. If you had committed a murder, the right Christian thing to do would be to give yourself up to the police and be hanged. It is, therefore, in my opinion, perfectly right for a Christian judge to sentence a man to death or a Christian soldier to kill an enemy. I always have thought so, ever since I became a Christian, and long before the war, and I think so now that we are at peace. It is no good quoting 'thou shall not kill.' There are two Greek words: the ordinary word to kill and the word to murder. And when Christ quotes that commandment He uses the murder one in all three accounts, Matthew, Mark, and Luke. ... All killing is not murder any more that all sexual intercourse is adultery.*

Was Jesus against Soldiers Performing Their Duty?

Jesus never suggested that serving in the military was against God's will. When a Roman Centurion came to him for healing of one of his servants, Jesus healed the servant and praised him because of his faith. Matthew 8:10 *"When Jesus heard this, he was amazed and said to those following him, "Truly I tell you, I have not found anyone in Israel with such great faith."* Later Cornelius, another Roman Centurion, was greeted by an angle who praised Cornelius. Peter visited his home and witnessed the Holy Spirit being poured out on Cornelius' family. Acts 10:22 *"The men replied, "We have come from Cornelius the centurion. He is a righteous and God-fearing man, who is respected by all the Jewish people. A holy angel told him to ask you to come to his house so that he could hear what you have to say."*

What Does the Bible say About Capital Punishment?

The Bible is clearly in favor of taking the life of a murderer:

1. Genesis 9:6 *"Whoever sheds human blood, by humans shall their blood be shed; for in the image of God has God made mankind.*

2. Exodus 21:12 *"Anyone who strikes a man and kills him shall surely be put to death.*

3. Numbers 35:16 *"If a man strikes someone with an iron object so that he dies, he is a murderer; the murderer shall be put to death.*

4. Romans 13:1 *"Let everyone be subject to the governing authorities, for there is no authority except that which God has established. The authorities that exist have been established by God."*

5. <u>Romans 13:3-4</u> *"For rulers hold no terror for those who do right, but for those who do wrong. Do you want to be free from fear of the one in authority? Then do what is right and he will commend you.* ⁴*For he is God's servant to do you good. But if you do wrong, be afraid, for he does not bear the sword for nothing. He is God's servant, an agent of wrath to bring punishment on the wrongdoer.*

6. <u>1st Peter 2:3</u> *"Submit yourselves for the Lord's sake to every authority instituted among men: whether to the king, as the supreme authority"*

Conclusion

God's Word makes it clear that the government has the God given right to capital punishment! The only exception to government using capital punishment is when it comes into direct conflict with God's Word.

CHAPTER 13

THE TRUTH WILL SET YOU FREE

Myth # 11: "Missions"… for Professionals Only

Definition of Missions

The word missions traditionally has been associated with the church's evangelistic outreach locally and to foreign lands. Mission's original focus has been on bringing people to a true knowledge of their sin and their essential need of forgiveness for their sins. Faith and belief in Jesus is man's only remedy from eternal separation from God in Hell. Jesus paid a steep price in order to pay in full for the punishment that our sins deserved. However, without knowledge of our sinfulness, man would not seek forgiveness and without knowledge of God's Savior, Jesus, man would be lost forever.

God's primary way of reaching His children is through other believers. All believers are to sow the seeds of faith and let God grow these seeds and draw His children to Him. This happens when new Christians receive His Holy Spirit and are "born again"..

God needs man to be the feet to carry His message to His Children.

<u>Romans 10:14-15</u> *"How, then, can they call on the one they have not believed in? And how can they believe in the one of whom they have not heard? And how can they hear without someone preaching to them?* [15] *And how can anyone preach unless they are sent? As it is written: "How beautiful are the feet of those who bring good news!"*

Many Christians today believe that mission work and evangelism should be left up to the professionals i.e. missionaries or clergy. This couldn't be farther from the truth. None of Jesus' original disciples were associated with the religious class. Only Paul, who joined the disciples after Jesus' resurrection, had any religious affiliation. However, Saul who later was named Paul was a Pharisee who persecuted Christians. After Paul's conversion by Jesus on the Damascus road, Paul became the greatest evangelist ever. Paul, rejected by the Jewish leaders, ministered to the Gentiles which opened up salvation to everyone worldwide who would believe in Him..

Our Battle is a Spiritual Battle

<u>Ephesians 6:12-13</u> *"For our struggle is not against flesh and blood, but against the rulers, against the authorities, against the powers of this dark world and against the spiritual forces of evil in the heavenly realms.* [13] *Therefore put on the full armor of God, so that when the day of evil comes, you may be able to stand your ground, and after you have done everything, to stand."* There is a battle going on in the heavenly realms that we do not see. It is between God and Satan's, spiritual forces of evil.

God's Holy Spirit enables Christians to resist Satan's seductive evil forces. <u>John 4:4</u> *"You, dear children, are from God and have overcome them, because the one who is in you is greater than the one who is in the world."* That doesn't mean that we won't sin anymore, but we know that God's mercy and grace are greater than our sins. Christians believe in God's promises of righteousness through the shed blood of Jesus, God's only Son.

God has Always Been Involved in Missions

The Scriptures reveal a God always active in mission beginning in Genesis. Mission begins in the heart of God and expresses his great love for the world. It is the Lord's gracious initiative and ongoing activity to save a world incapable of saving itself. Genesis 12:1-3 *"The LORD had said to Abram, "Go from your country, your people and your father's household to the land I will show you. ² "I will make you into a great nation, and I will bless you; I will make your name great, and you will be a blessing. ³ I will bless those who bless you, and whoever curses you I will curse; and all peoples on earth will be blessed through you."* Forty one hundred years later Jesus commanded His disciples, a group of fishermen, a tax collector and a doctor, to go and make disciples of all nations. Matthew 28:19-20 *"Therefore go and make disciples of all nations, baptizing them in the name of the Father and of the Son and of the Holy Spirit, ²⁰ and teaching them to obey everything I have commanded you. And surely I am with you always, to the very end of the age."*

Man's salvation is entirely from God, who through Christ reconciled us to himself and gave us the ministry of reconciliation. Therefore, all believers are ambassadors for Christ weather paid clergy or lay persons. God makes His appeal to the lost through every believer. Mark 16:15-16 *"He said to them, "Go into all the world and preach the gospel to all creation. ¹⁶ Whoever believes and is baptized will be saved, but whoever does not believe will be condemned."*

Since all unbelievers, will be condemned eternally, shouldn't every believer make an effort to explain the importance of the Gosple to their family and friends? God will eventually bring His mission to completion on the day Christ returns to judge both the living and the dead. God will gather all believers to himself and send the rest to eternal damnation. God's loving patience delays judgement so that the Gospel might be preached throughout the world. Matthew 24:14 *"And this gospel of the kingdom will be preached in the whole world as a testimony to all nations, and then the end will come."*

Sin is the Problem

The harmony that originally characterized God's created order has also been disrupted by sin. We live in a fallen world where, instead of peace and love, sins like lust and greed, hatred and jealousy, domination and exploitation wound and destroy. All sins of thought, word, and deed bring pain and grief into human relationships, and also ruin the harmony between human beings and nature.

Most dreadful of all the consequences of sin is that it "condemns us to the eternal wrath of God all those who are not "born again." Those through faith who have received God's Holy Spirit. As unpleasant and unpopular as they may be, these sobering realities of sin and God's wrath must be faced and confessed in order for us to recognize the necessity and urgency of God's rescue mission in Christ. John 3:18 ***"Whoever believes in him is not condemned, but whoever does not believe stands condemned already because they have not believed in the name of God's one and only Son."***

The creation itself was "subjected to futility" so that it knows only a "bondage to decay" and is "groaning in travail" under the burden of sin. Romans 8:19-22 ***"For the creation waits in eager expectation for the children of God to be revealed. 20 For the creation was subjected to frustration, not by its own choice, but by the will of the one who subjected it, in hope 21 that the creation itself will be liberated from its bondage to decay and brought into the freedom and glory of the children of God. 22 We know that the whole creation has been groaning as in the pains of childbirth right up to the present time."***

Before sin came into the world, God's creation was perfect with harmony, peace and there was no death or decay. Once sin entered the world, it spread like a plague and affected everyone. God intervened numerous times in order to limit sin from spreading throughout the Old Testament. God's greatest interdiction was His great flood saving only Noah and his family. God also prevented all the adult Israelites who doubted God's ability to lead the people into the "Promise Land", they all died in the desert. Only Joshua and Caleb who believed in God's ability to and give them the land He promised Abraham survived the 40 years of wandering in the desert..

God is Omniscient but Satan is Not

God is omniscient so he knows who his children or followers are. You are either lost or saved, a believer or an antichrist! Jesus, the good Shepard, knows His children and they know Him! John 10:14 *"I am the good shepherd; I know my sheep and my sheep know me—"* John 10:4-5 *"When he has brought out all his own, he goes on ahead of them, and his sheep follow him because they know his voice. ⁵ But they will never follow a stranger; in fact, they will run away from him because they do not recognize a stranger's voice."* It is up to us to get God's message of redemption out to all His Children. Since we are not to judge because only God knows Man's heart, we must spread God's message of redemption to everyone.

Satan has many powers but unlike God he does not know who his children or followers are. Therefore, Satan uses the shotgun approach and tries to influence everyone by bending God's truth in order to mislead as many people astray as possible. He also attacks wherever he see the "Churches" strengths i.e. Catholic Priests, TV Evangelists, and all who are being successful in spreading God's message of salvation..

Satan has taken over the Mid-East which was mainly Christian at one time. Today most of the people living there are Moslems. In this country, Satan has been very successful removing God from our public schools and universities; he has major influence with the main line media and he has even infiltrated many of our churches.

Believers should not get discouraged as God is in complete control and He knows even the number of hairs on our head. God will reach every one of "His Children" no matter where they live through other missions. Remember, the thief on the cross was saved in the last minutes of his life and that possibility is available to others.

God's Mission is My Mission

The mission God gives to the whole church he also gives to each individual member of the church. In Holy Baptism God adopted each of us by name into his family, and called us to be involved personally in the task of reaching out to all people with his saving Gospel message. Jesus' call to discipleship is "Follow me!" This Gospel message applies to each one of us, and by granting us the privilege of carrying our own cross for His sake and the Gospel's.

Our personal involvement in God's mission takes place wherever we are—wherever God has placed us. Each of us is called to serve God and bear witness to his grace whether as child, parent, husband, wife, citizen, employee, employer, government official, soldier, police officer, teacher, construction worker. As we serve faithfully "as to the Lord", opportunities will arise to testify by word and deed to the hope that is within us as a result of our faith in Jesus Christ.

What Should Believers Strive to Do?

As individual members of the body of Christ and by the power of the Holy Spirit, we are to Strive:

1. To live the new life, which God's Spirit enables us to live, be "born again".

2. To share, at every opportunity, the message of God's mercy and grace for sinners which includes everyone. .

3. To be nurtured in our relationship with God through regular and diligent searching of the Scriptures.

4. To pray continually for God's Kingdom to come and his will to be done.

5. To make the most of every opportunity to "do good to all especially to those who are of the household of faith"

6. To identify and encourage qualified individuals for professional service in God's church, even as we ourselves eagerly respond to God's call, saying here am I! Send me

Each of us has received from God's hand grace upon grace, all flowing from the sacrificial service of the One who laid down his life for us on the cross. We cannot, therefore, leave the work of God's mission to "the church" in general or to "others" who may appear more gifted for the task or to "the pastors." What an honor it is to follow in the footsteps of God's Servant-Son, and to share with others the love he has so freely and fully bestowed on us! Each of us is a personal letter from Christ to the world.

As we strive to carry out faithfully the mission mandate of our Lord, we are comforted, refreshed and strengthened by the assurance that the mission is *the Lord's*. Although he has entrusted it to us, he continues to guide and direct it, sustains it with his presence and promises, and empowers it by providing the divine means through which the mission accomplishes its divine purposes.

BIBLIOGRAPHY

Luther, Martin. *THE BONDAGE OF THE WILL.* Grand Rapids: Flemming H. Revell, 1957.

MacArthur, John. *THE GOSPEL ACCORDING TO JESUS.* Grand Rapids: Zondervan, 2008.

Mac Arthur, John. *HARD TO BELIEVE.* Nashville: Thomas Nelson, Inc., 2003

Lewis, C.S. *MERE CHRISTIANITY.* New York: Harper Collins, 2001

DeYoung, Dr. Don, *THOUSANDS...NOT BILLIONS.* Green Forest: Master Books, 2005

Woodward, Thomas. *DOUBTS ABOUT DARWIN.* Grand Rapids: Baker Books, 2003

Barker, Kenneth. *THE NIV STUDY BIBLE.* Grand Rapids: Zondervan, 1995

Walther, C. F. W. *LAW & GOSPEL.* St Louis: Concordia Publishing House, 2010